DRAPING THE SKY FOR A SNOWFALL

Julian Wolfreys

Published by:
Triarchy Press
Axminster, England

info@triarchypress.net
www.triarchypress.net

Copyright © Julian Wolfreys, 2016

The right of Julian Wolfreys to be identified as the author of this work has been asserted by him in accordance with the Copyright, Designs and Patents Act, 1988

No part of this publication may be reproduced, stored in a retrieval system or transmitted in any form or by any means including photocopying, electronic, mechanical, recording or otherwise, without the prior written permission of the publisher.

All rights reserved

A catalogue record for this book is available from the British Library.

Print ISBN: 978-1-909470-94-1
ePub ISBN: 978-1-909470-95-8

The cricketer has his Wisden,
The pilot has got his Jane's;
The sum of this factual wisdom
Won't help us to fly the 'plane.
(No, and it never will.)

– Peter Hammill

For

Brian Hinton

ACKNOWLEDGEMENTS

Paintings: Judy Rodrigues
Photographs: Monika Szuba and Julian Wolfreys

It is always impossible to judge the right thing to say regarding acknowledgements. The question is one of gratitude, but also of debt.

There is always a shadow of the economic behind any response, in the calculation of what might be the right thing to say. It is impossible to know the right thing.

There is no right thing. Silence is not an option either.

In the words of Samuel Beckett, words that are applicable in so many situations, trivial or grave, I can't go on, I'll go on.

Thank you, to Andrew Carey, for having the vision, the interest, the care. And thank you too, Andrew, for the words of inquiry, encouragement, wit and bemused bafflement – oh, yes, and that particular, peripatetic bird.

Thank you, Catherine Bernard and Jean-Michel Rabaté for offering thoughts on my French translations; thank you Doris Bremm for checking my German. Thank you to Birgit van Puymbroeck and Tone Selboe for your translations of 'Logos' into Dutch and Norwegian respectively.

Thank you, Judy Rodrigues for permission to use your paintings and sketches that were conceived and realised at Ventnor Botanic Gardens.

Thank you, Monika Szuba, thank you, so much, for your irreplaceable, essential Polish translations.

CONTENTS

Acknowledgements	5
Foreword – J. Hillis Miller	11
Preface	15
SUN WAN SKY WASTED / Place	16
MILK PAINTS MAGPIE WHITE Grief	18
YOU ARE / Subject	20
WIDMOLOGIA / Untitled	22
SUN DRIED / Being	24
NOTHING TO BE DONE / Appropriation	28
GOOD FRIDAY / Untitled	28
JIM AND SUE / Moments	32
UP AT JACK'S / Balloon	36
SUB ROSA / Untitled	38
PROSERPINA SLEEPS / Khora	42
STIMMUNGSTRÄGER / Bird Traps and Lighthouses	44
CORVID / The Undecidable	48
SONG / Arbitrary	48
ULYSSES ON THE NORTHERN SHORE / Untitled	52
A DAY / Reclamation	54
DRAPING THE SKY FOR A SNOWFALL (LÜBECK)	58
NAMELESS / Untitled	64
FORGET ME NOT / The Mouse's Ear	66
REPRESENTATIONS / The Uncountable	68
THERE IS THIS / Untitled	68
SCENTED / As If	72
THE VILLAGE / Community	74
BALTIC CORRESPONDANCE / Bałtycka Korespondencja	76
1. An Armful, Yours / Naręcze, Twoje	76
2. Baltic / Bałtyk	78

3. You Send Me Photographs / Przysyłasz Mi Zdjęcia	80
4. Barn Owl and Fox Glove / Płomykówka I Naparstnica	82
5. Sehnsucht/ Sehnsucht	84
6. Read / Czytaj	88
7. You, Remain	88
8. Road / Droga	92
9. A Miller's Tale / Opowieść Młynarza	94
10. Kashubia / Kaszuby	96
11. Owl and Mullein / Sówka I Dziewanna	98
12. Chauchat Triptych / Tryptyk Chauchat	98
13. Same Sky / To Samo Niebo	102
14. Proper Names / Nazwy Własne	104
THE POET, TRANSLATED / Untitled	106
HERBSTFREUDE / A Beautiful Day	108
POPPY / Memory	110
JOSEFKA / Untitled	112
SLEEP, THE SEA / Teal? Teal!	114
THE ART OF TRANSLATION / Lequel? Laquelle?	116
THE FUR TRADER AND THE POET / Untitled	118
MIRABELKA AT THE BEACH / Imagine (or, the Truth otherwise told)	120
1. A Calendar of Convergences	122
2. The Olive Park	122
3. A Different Beach	124
4. Mirabelka	130
PŁOMYKÓWKA / Animalallegory	132
EN ATTENDANT QUIPROQUO / Untitled	134
LOGOS / What's the Word?	136
MOURNING / Of Love and other ghosts	142
Afterword – Jean-Michel Rabaté	177

FOREWORD

Secrets ... Ellipses

> It is said that the dead are the most demanding of our love. We are defenceless and delinquent in the face of them.
>
> (Wolfreys, *Silent Music*)

> You risked everything on this quotation: "The work of love in recollecting the one who is dead is the work of the most disinterested, free, and faithful love". It is signed: ... For your name? No, you never did that. For the author then, someone you had read; whom I cannot recall ....
>
> (Wolfreys, *Silent Music*)

Draping the Sky for a Snowfall moves me greatly. It shows that Julian Wolfreys is an extremely distinguished poet. Wolfreys is also many other things: a spectacular musician (player of many instruments, composer, lyricist, arranger, performer, recording artist); a brilliant and exceptionally learned scholar (for example in his multivolume account of those who have written about life in London); a creative editor (of a series on Victorian literature and culture for Edinburgh University Press); a publisher and editor, a gifted organizer of conferences (for example one some years ago now at Loughborough University on 'Rural Experience'); a wonderful writer of fiction (in *Silent Music*). How does he find time and creative energy to do all these things? He is a prodigy. I was familiar with all these gifts except, until recently, his gift for poetry. I might have known!

How can I say anything that will help you to read *Draping the Sky for a Snowfall*? Not easy. You must in the end read it for yourself, make what you can for yourself of these poems. I have put them in my title under the aegis of 'secrets' and 'ellipses'. 'Secrets' for their 'hermeneutical' side, what is meant, *das Gemeinte*; 'ellipses' for their 'poetics' side, *die Art des Meinens*, the way meanings are expressed. In this case that means how the secrets are eloquently written about, while at the same time being kept. *Draping the Sky* is elliptical in both meaning and poetics. It sometimes seems as if Wolfreys is trying to see how much he can leave out and still have his readers feel they are idiots if they cannot figure out *das Gemeinte*, what is meant. There are reasons for his elliptical reticence.

Many of these poems concern an ethical duty: the speaker's endless and unfulfillable obligation to render justice to the dead beloved. He must do that as much as anything by remembering her as clearly as possible: her laugh, her smile, her body, the silent looks they exchanged, events of bodily touching. On the other hand, many of these poems celebrate the idea of the beloved. The same? another? It is impossible to tell. It remains what Derrida would call an undecidable. Whoever the speaker might be – and there is no reason to assume that the author and the speaker are one – Wolfreys' poems strive again and again to understand, from the perspective of whatever moment he writes a poem now, what occurs in an event, a crisis, and how to bear witness, to find adequate words for it.

Wolfreys' conceptual presuppositions are made clear by way of repeated and varied formulations. A particularly explicit formulation is 'Read', a poem in the section called 'Baltic Correspondance'. The other person, the beloved, even in moments of greatest intimacy remains wholly other, unreachable, untouchable, secret. Death does no more than seal, once and for all, the otherness of the beloved. Each poem is therefore:

> A song that speaks of everything
> In secret, in unspoken words,
> And otherwise,
> An afterword
> An other's tongue

The conceptual aporia of these poems is evident. As the poem cycle titled 'Mourning' reveals, not to speak of the dead is to betray an exigent responsibility. To speak of the dead adequately is, however, impossible. Any words for this eternal secret are a betrayal. To speak of it is to traduce it. Not to speak of it is to traduce it. Either way you have had it big time. Wolfreys' poems hover eloquently within this impasse.

Paradoxically, the aporia of the other's permanently secret otherness does not generate silence but lots of powerful poems that speak of it 'otherwise', in displaced figures or, properly speaking, catachreses. This may be the reason Wolfreys is so chary about anchoring events. One poem speaks of a lighthouse. Which lighthouse, exactly? That remains a secret.

I have cited in my two epigraphs Wolfreys' *Silent Music*, which tells in lyrical prose the narrative of a love and a loss. Who knows the extent of fiction in this novel, or to what extent anything – if anything – might have some factual or historical referent. In any case, if Wolfreys had wanted to show his hand, had he wanted the readers of his poems to know that facts there were, he presumably would have made this clear. Were the novel in any way factual, Wolfreys would doubtless have referred those readers to *Silent Music* somewhere in *Draping the Sky for a Snowfall*. There is a thematic sympathy between the poems and the novels to be sure, but not necessarily a connection. Since he does not make connections, I think it is better not to know *Silent Music* exists or at least to pretend not to know and not to use it in explanation or presumption of missing facts. The danger of knowing 'the facts behind', as Wolfreys no doubt realized, is that autobiographical explanations tend to inhibit actual reading. You say, 'Oh, I see. It's a transcription of his life. Then I don't need to read the poems carefully, just learn about the facts of his life'.

The hermeneutical meaning of *Draping the Sky* is clear enough, though some filling in of blanks and connecting of dots may be necessary to extrapolate clear meaning from what is often expressed elliptically and indirectly. What about the poetics of *Draping the Sky*, however, *die Art des Meinen*? It would seem at first that the poetical devices Wolfreys employs are just the right ones for expressing the hermeneutical meaning he wants to convey. These are modes of radical ambiguity that are especially common in some modern American poetry (which may not have influenced Wolfreys one bit, for all I know): William Carlos Williams, Gertrude Stein, Louis Zukovsky, Charles Olson, or the Language poets. These features of ellipsis are also already there in Mallarmé or Rimbaud.

I list some: short lines that make a phrase or word hang in the air detached from what would syntactically complete it: momentarily at least, the fragment hides its secret (an example is the words 'A secret' that make a whole line in 'Up at Jack's'); wordplay with words that have contradictory meanings, sometimes non-English words, as in the fun Wolfreys has with the word *Vorspiel*, which can mean the beginning section of a piece of music or of some other composition, but also sexual foreplay, as in the tongue-kissing Wolfreys' speaker bears witness to; play with ambiguous pronouns, I, you, he, she, we, those 'floating signifiers'; incomplete sentences; unexplained allusions, citations, or place-names; untranslated words in some foreign language, as in the bits of German, French, and Latin, or the Polish interpellations and translations throughout the section 'Baltic Correspond*a*nce'. (Note that italicized *a*: has another tongue taken over, is this now French? or is this another of Wolfreys' elliptical allusions, some indirect reference to the *a* of Derridean *différance*? This is entirely likely, knowing Wolfreys, but it remains impossible to tell. Though a thought occurs; perhaps, given the playfulness, Wolfreys' French spelling also tells the reader that there is a *dance* between lovers here.) The Polish is wholly opaque to me, its meaning hidden. Such devices successfully hide their secrets. That is what Wolfreys' speaker says he must do vis-à-vis the beloved (however many, or few, there are), so poetics happily matches hermeneutics.

On the other hand, and finally, such devices are not just ways of speaking otherwise about the secrecy of the other person, alive or dead. A word or phrase just hanging in the air, like Wolfreys' other poetic devices, is, strictly speaking, not a rich ambiguity but just plain meaningless. It does not aid Wolfreys one bit in getting his hermeneutical meaning stated clearly. *Die Art des Meinens* turns into *Die Art des Sinnlosigkeit*, the art of meaninglessness; or, if you prefer one of these translations: futility, absurdity, hollowness, senselessness, pointlessness, purposelessness, meaninglessness. Ultimately perhaps just loss. Reading Wolfreys' ellipses is like reading *Heart of Darkness*, as if it were written by Beckett, not Conrad.

I do not feel that my Foreword has got matters much 'forrader', as we say in the United States, that is, much further forward. My advice: ignore what I have said (which you can hardly do if you have already read it far enough to get to my disclaimer). In any case, forget it. Better to read these wonderfully melodious and powerful poems for yourself and in your own way. Reading them has been a great, but troubling, delight for me.

J. Hillis Miller

Incidental narratives, emerging only after the event, as the memory's web of traces shape the details into something more apparently meaningful, call for a greater significance than they really have. This happens all the time, even though the chance concatenation always has the uncanny resonance of revenant arrival. The temptation to seek for, and find, patterns in the random remains a temptation not to be resisted. Apophenia: the goddess of meaningful and desiring perception.

PREFACE

Two books in one place, the one blind to the other; the other, regarding askance, obliquely, and as it were on occasion, slyly the steps being taken, retraced, the motions and dances, the hesitancies of all that you will find on the left-hand, the verso, as you are looking, and it is to be hoped, reading one or the other, one after the other. *Nacheinander. Nebeneinander.* German words and therefore, clearly, not mine. Meaning, on the one hand, one after the other, while, on the other hand, one next to the other. These words are found, fragments of a foreign tongue, awash in the mouth perhaps, but certainly in the mind of an Irish student, recalled home from study in Paris, at the death of his mother. Thus, these words are not his either. Found scraps, expressing spatial and temporal relations, which the student takes up, while walking along the strand, on a beach, a pebbly surface, uneven in such a way as to make one aware of every step, one after, one next to the other. It is as if these found words have been washed up on the shoreline of a smaller island somewhere off the greater coast of a larger island, itself adjacent to a continent of tongues, washed and carried across the sea.

Words, never ours, arrive, and if we are fortunate, we find momentary employment for them. Some rougher, some smoothed, each with its own measure, weight, density. All have drifted, regardless of borders, to tumble, and populate for a time divers mouths, countless pages, a heterogeneity of tongues. Inmixing, commingling with what is presumed local, but which in many cases is merely an older deposit, already tongue-knotted with different traces.

Stories, poems, like roads, take unexpected turns. We find ourselves moving in directions never planned. Travelling, the driver will find himself confronted with an unexpected association, a memory, an animal in the headlights. Names, initials, sigla, the irrealities of the familiar and everyday, jostle within, alongside, at night particularly, where the strangeness of casual substitution assumes a greater apparent significance, metaphor, metonymy, synecdoche giving way to a deliberate, and therefore wilful catachresis. In truth such odd substitution waits on, attendant on the moment of its unexpected arrival, the merest moment in which it comes to give pause, bring to a halt, slam on the brakes. But convergences happen, chance encounters the result of a stranger's idiocy, coming to pass at just that moment, when passing below, the uninvited stranger is called on by the event to make a decision in the face of a crisis, altruism the belated name applied.

The result, a late night ride, private rather than public transport. Memory and narrative do not meet up however, do not come to arrive, until, chance playing its part (as in all good stories, all poetic drives), a point in the same road is passed through once more, at night again. The events recalled, the moment is later written down. Another drive, another instant of coincidence and collision, memory meeting memory, and the revelation that here again, here we were, in the car, though we no longer necessarily steer. Let go the wheel, allow the motion to carry you. We all travel, waiting for the revelation at the curve.

SUN WAN SKY WASTED

It was late autumn; sun wan sky wasted day.
A figure coming into view, from out Knowles Copse,
The bay behind, horseshoe shod,
A susurration stirring in the marshes

A tall figure, a player of strings,
A weaver of wool, and songs,
And stories tripping tongue laughingly along;
A cellist with a butterfly net
That October afternoon heading home

Skin, light-henna brown, nutmeg soft and furred,
All but imperceptible, but giving to the touch

She would sing, regardless of the world,
Seasonal counterpoints, of rosebuds in June
The times of year all contretemps,
As, widdershins, she turned, dancing,
To the rhythm of her own melodic lilt and lay.

I saw that. Once.
I see it now, once more

Again I see her laughter's ripple
Unselfconscious on the air,
A sound thin threaded with ale and wine,
Cheese and apples on the tongue
Spittle shared, and closer than myself

I taste again the absence of a heart
Unadorned and bared to all the world,
Defiant of mortality.

Each place has its own time. Gathering time into it, the identity of place is assumed over time, as each successive epoch gives way to another, without being wholly erased in the process. So, one location may contain more than a millennium in its existence. What the eye sees is thus more than what is present, more than what is visible. For what is seen in the present has been determined by successive instances of transformation in each and every past, then and now perceived, felt, though not wholly apprehended. One looks unseeing onto the past in the field of vision, within which are memory's invisibles.

There has been a Knowles Farm for several centuries. The buildings surviving date from the 17th century. They reflect a polyfocal distribution pattern typical for the time; and equally typically for the area, the house has a stone and thatch lobby. Away from the farm, toward the bay, sloping toward Brading Marshes and Bembridge Lagoons, Knowles Copse remains, a distinctive feature, with noticeable groupings of silver leaved poplars, which would have been visible from the train, when the branch line reached its terminus on Station Road, adjacent to the harbour. South of Embankment Roads, the copse is what remains of a prehistoric woodland. To the west of the copse, beyond the farm, is Bembridge Windmill. Built around the beginning of the eighteenth century, it was, and remains, known by some as Knowles Windmill, although owned and operated by the Dennetts. J. M. W. Turner painted the four-storey structure in 1795. The mill's wooden cap could be turned on a continuous chain, in order that the sails might be turned to face into the wind.

Widdershins: an old word, barely used, though associated with Scots dialect. As with landscapes, its history is encrypted; arriving from another tongue early in the sixteenth century, and another age, its source Middle High German, meaning 'against' (*wider*) and 'direction' (*sin*). Alternatively, the German source might be *widersinnig*, translatable as 'against sense'. The motion it names is counter-clockwise, a course contrary to the movement of the sun. Language may indeed work 'against sense', it is not always the function of language to convey meaning unequivocally. Even in those places where the signification seems apparent, transparent, without explanation, so there may be within, underneath the skin of that word, the tongue of the other articulating in a whisper, barely that, a sense that goes against the commonly accepted sense.

MILK PAINTS MAGPIE WHITE

You spill.
Hand thrown, a careless arc of grief
Across and out
Stone skimming water's tense

A cup is caught, a glass upends,
Down and out, away, unfilling liquid
Of a memory's tidal pool

Milk paints magpie white
The tiles, a jet
That, nearer blue than black,
Bruise breaking bent,
A stroke that paints
Her lost love's laugh

Forming,
So deep a sound
So swift a flight

From you, a fallward failure
Of limbs in cutup catechism
Readymade

Outwith the shake and stutter,
Shudder halts a time-lapse tear
Reversing dryness,
Creep guilty to the duct,
Draping the sky for a snowfall

There is always a negotiation to be experienced, and so felt, between memory and history. The needs, the desires of the one maintain a tension, sometimes in concert, at other times in resistance, reaction or opposition to the demands of the other. Memory can always speak to perception and feeling, indeed it frequently does. History on the other hand seeks to resist such failures and excesses. Memory, however, has its registers, its modes of recollection, representation and acts of attestation, wherein there can appear a sense of dramatic irony, which historical narrative can – and often does – overlook, save for the rhetorical flourish on the part of the self-aware historian. Memory, meanwhile, apprehends the rhetorical, the poetic, as of its very utterance, the medium of the weave itself, the only means by which the places of the past come to have their chance of returning, and so, of speaking performatively for themselves. What is once, is now again, in memory, albeit of a different order, there being no presence to the illusory present given momentary form. What was witnessed at one time can never be witnessed again, as such. History's narratives assume the opposite, and there is in the recounting of history a tacit suggestion that the gap between the now of the writer and the now of the event (and the now of the reader, it has to be said) might be closed.

How to read trauma, its experience, its signs, symptoms? These are not the questions of the analyst. Nor should the answers be taken as self-evident. Trauma may play itself out, repeat itself in numerous ways, interpreting, translating the effects on which it relies, so the questions become fundamental. Such questions are always in the experience of the subject, as a matrix of traces that iterate and tattoo themselves in the subject.

Trauma, its afterlife, is, as emotion or affect, the encounter with phenomena, the apophatic or analogical revenance that is felt, then narrated, often otherwise. If experience of the everyday is semantic, if the tales we recount of our daily lives are narrative, then the articulation of trauma in the body is semiotic, poetic, in which the gaps are as significant as the signs. Memory can make claims on us in unreasonable and exorbitant, unexpected ways. Grief is never reasonable or tidy. Anguish can reach such a pitch as to break through words to physical, corporeal articulation.

The body becomes rewritten by a language, several tongues, various registers all its own, yet also foreign. Unable any longer to bear the burden, corporeality succumbs to behaviour, affect, demeanour that is neither simply conscious nor unconscious but defamiliarised, as if one were to find oneself, albeit belatedly, engaged in a parodic performance of oneself.

Time's measure is changed, distorted, felt in different measures, alternating tempi, according to the regions of the body in the act translated. Grief, from the Old French, *grever* (to burden), speaks of the physical immensity, of a great weight, which trauma metaphorises, bringing to bear a psychic materiality, as real as any material object. This weight appears in the subject as a force, the imagined materiality of the psychic burden is phantomised in the event of the unanticipated, often wordless, though not inarticulate corporeal confession.

Memory, though, admits a space, places a gap between one moment and another, one experience and another. In so doing, memory doubles rather than offering a mere mimetically faithful representation. Memory says of the trace that articulates its each, singular instance: I see the event, I am in it. The *I* belongs to the event, which returns to dwell within the subject in a fashion that is reciprocal, allowing the subject to see and feel the ghostly encounter.

Impossible to close, Mnemosyne's chasm can affect intimately, can open suddenly and with a pull impossible to measure. The pleasure, the *frisson*, reveals to the subject the ability of the dead to have a more real afterlife in their posthumous effect, than was possible in the instant of the past – because the day to day obscures in any instant, through habit, a closeness, and the affect thereof, for which history has no use, but for which it cannot account or admit in its restricted economy. Pleasure or sadness: history has no place in its discourse for them, except as objects of its forensic inquiry, striving to inoculate itself against all that is other.

YOU ARE

You are
Decidedly
Of the islands.

A Voice not my own.

This drifts,
A focus: a sound on air,
Interrupted.

You, A flower
Sitting brightly.

Another figure disrupts
What should be
Private, intimate.

Surrounded

This other, this obvious
Intrusion

By sounds and sweet airs
That delight and hurt not.

Another's words
So much historical driftwood

SUBJECT

When we engage with fictive texts, proper names and place names are important. The proper name of a street, of a church or park, an area of a town – all such proper names act in a text as locators for the reader. 'Mappable' co-ordinates for the imagination, they translate between an imagined real world and the projection of world in which the mind engages when reading: topography become discourse in fixed points suggestive of space-become-place, and so returned in reading to the material. Defined, finite, apprehended through the medium of writing. Verisimilitude takes place as a staging effect, encoded in the act of writing, representation at work where name serves to knit the imaginary substrate that we might perceive as the world.

The text arrives as a reading of imagined location. There on the page, the points of reference, even the most minimal – the allusion to islands, with that self-reflexive citation and the more indirect figure of driftwood – presents a ground for whatever passes as action, narrative, event. However minimal, there arrive points of light, compass markers of orientation and illumination. I, You, He, She serve similar functions: these move – have always already moved – into their particular assigned locations, characters on a stage, voices enacting the self and world, to move once more in the act of reading, to assume for the reader the work of mapping and staging.

This is, to be sure, a representational function, but a function that serves in the greater generation of significance according to the relation of the parts to the whole.

Voices appear, to be heard. How many? Can they be counted? A speaker addresses another figure, though who this is remains enigmatic. A line appears, on its own, acknowledging a voice distinct from its own. Is this one of the first two. Two voices. Or are there more? Not explicitly in opposition, for only one seems to know the other is there, although there is also, depending on how one counts, a dim perception of another. Are we in the presence of something being acted out? Where there is voice, there theatre takes place. This is a theatre of voices, an undifferentiated space, unnamed, place barely discernible. The reader has reference to islands; this is echoed further in that conscious allusion to *The Tempest*, a play about magic, power, politics, and, of course, theatricality. Does this reveal anything though? Or is it one more layer of obfuscation. The reader is aware of a critical consciousness becoming apparent to itself at the beginning – this is the condition of theatre, the theatre of Being and the being of theatre. As soon as there is voice, there is consciousness; wherefore consciousness, therefore reflection; in reflection, the performance, hence theatre. The self, this commentator on what might be called the 'first', the inaugural voice, enters the stage. Here though, voices without bodies. Unincorporated. The appearance is of drifting consciousness, voices recollecting the event, unnamed yet placed. There is tension in the shift, between the shafts of observation and exposition. Ariel, maintaining surveillance, sees and comments.

Place, name, pronominal indicator in writing do not merely correspond to an external location, a terrain. Place is no simple backdrop. A material terrain, real or fictive, has a corresponding inner map, a psychic set of co-ordinates that are aligned, or become engaged through what takes place in the narrative situated in the material site. There must, therefore, be a mode of play, of motion or torque between the literal and the figurative that withholds and reveals simultaneously, in tension and flux, point and counterpoint, the narrative and dramatic focus, upon which the reader should come, as it were in an instant of revelation.

WIDMOLOGIA

The season, in advance of itself,
Confused above and below,
Not quite, though anticipating, autumn,
The air transparent with expectation:
The sweet soft unseen future
Somewhere between the trees
Across the road's rumour,
Borne by the scents of beeches,
The damper, the darker.

Entering the neighbour's meadow,
Crossing, anticipation rife, steps tentative,
Though swift toward an older mystery.
Moving as a child, with childlike faith,
– *Magike Tekhne* – we passed,
Willing the suspension of fears,
In the acceptance of a darkness,
Welcoming at the edge.

If you looked to the soil, the day remained.
If you glanced at the sky, the night began.
In between, there, pausing, stepping, not,
Though then again, a ritual of delight,
Entangled with a greater anticipation.
Beech gives way, the motion sure, to Spruce,
Impossibly tall, shutting out the light,
Some dark, some almost sleeptime black,
Trunks overturned, their insides facing out,
Deep hollows, branches wound, embracing their own kind.

In the city still, at early morning,
Or waiting for the sun to disappear,
The sky to calm, mechanical adumbrations
Giving place to the baized fur of twilight,
Within unseen, a last avian cry draws once more
Upon my other child's self,
Forest time speaks, whistling
– *Vissla*, says another tongue carried east
From the further shore of my nearer sea –
Forming somewhere, buried deep,
This unspeaking being at my heart.
The roots, thread doubling, within
To call at fingers' end, ravelling me back,
unstitching my older contours,
Plaiting, willow woven – there, another Baltic sound
Transmigrating: *vika!*
This forest child, without words
Who keeps my truer secrets.

SUN DRIED

Standing sun faced, blind
August overheated, parching,
No focus, no attention,
Drawn nowhere by design

Sun dried, salt gathering
Here, and there, sea emerged,
Salt rime, tasted at the shoulder
Tanned and tired

Captured by indifference,
One ear given to a buzzing
Overhead drone, too lazy,
Too insistent

        Slow and low

Though far away

The day crawls
With memories of
Clare, Blake, Housman;
Of the pick, puck, pock:
Willow sounding in the sun for six,
Harper drifting through it all

A vision of Albion remembered,
One of those days in England
Another of those days

– There's an angel standing in the sun
Said Peter

White on green,
A tidied nostalgia
Suffused with the lust of an elderly poet

In all of which, there

        There

A vision, a visionary
        Glimpse
The secret, sensual, in full view
Vouchsafed

    Remaining

[continues

BEING

Being, in phenomenological thought, is inseparable from the world. The world that I see is my world in that the exteriority of the world (which I perceive to be a constellation of objects and phenomena) is not separate, fundamentally from the interiority of the self, wherein I 'think' the world that I perceive. Being and World are coextensive, not separate.

A limit however arrives in certain strands of phenomenological discourse around the question of the erotic relation between self and other, spoken of by Jean-Luc Marion. Problems with the word 'commerce' in relation to the erotic aside, as the good Derridean (I believe myself to be), I am struck by the aporia, a philosophical paradox nestled at the heart of Marion's otherwise flawless materialist phenomenology of the erotic phenomenon. For he fails to realise that in every utterance of the phrase 'my flesh' (Ma chair), he names without naming, the other, or at the very least admits the other's phantasmic 'penetration' of Being, of the subject (and also, I would problematise at the very least, were there space, the unthinking phallogocentrism of the invasive war-economy at play in the tropes of penetration). For when I say 'ma chair', is it my flesh, which I am naming, this flesh I think of as 'mine', and not merely this chance corporeality that embodies the I that thinks and reflects, or is it yours? To say 'my flesh' may be a phrase naming my own corporeality, or it may announce my sense of possessing the other's flesh, as though I had a right to it. Moreover, there is an ambiguity here in that when I utter the phrase, am I calling you 'my flesh' or am I responding to you, that which I believe to be my flesh (yours possessed by me is mine), imagining you, flesh of my flesh (the theological priority of the one is always already deconstructed by the call of the other) as the other already within, in the most intimate and spectral fashion, which awaits no penetration? In responding to, affirming, confessing the other, bearing witness to the other's always already having arrived, I have been opened by the other, revealed within myself as having, through the grace of the other's ghostly touch to which I can attest with every absence, been freed from the constraints of Being's privative horizon. Inasmuch as I welcome or become aware of the other, I am always already responding, I am in response, answering yes to the other's being-there.

> "Being... limits me, a horizon in the strict sense, a horizon by definition finite. Being finitises me according to its essential finitude. It holds me and restrains me. In order to get myself out and away, it is necessary that my flesh enter into commerce with another flesh.... I can only free myself and become myself by touching another flesh, as one touches land at a port, because only another flesh can make room for me, welcome me, and not turn away or resist me.... And where would the other flesh make a place for mine, if not *within itself*? Since the world makes no room, another flesh must do it for me.... I feel, all at once, both my flesh and the other flesh, by feeling that it cannot resist against me, that it wants not to resist me, that it takes me in its place without comprehending me there.... By entering into the flesh of the other, I exit the world and I become flesh in her flesh, flesh *of* her flesh. The other gives me to myself for the first time, because she takes the initiative to give me my own flesh for the first time. She awakens me."
>
> (Jean-Luc Marion, *Le phénomène érotique*, 118-19; translation mine.)

The imprint gone from a lavender field –
Buds crushed by summer's desire, impromptu
Hidden from view,
The scent of flowers fully formed,
Blossoming archly,
    The spine reaching up,
        To curve away from damper earth
Bees scenting the honey yet to come
Richstickythick, birdlime viscid
Slow, reaching,
Finger to finger,
Tongue on tongue

– Mneme, a body blow to travel at full tilt
Which bends and bows, but does not break
The older body's recollection.

The richness of archaic words

No longer used, but appealing to any who might hear

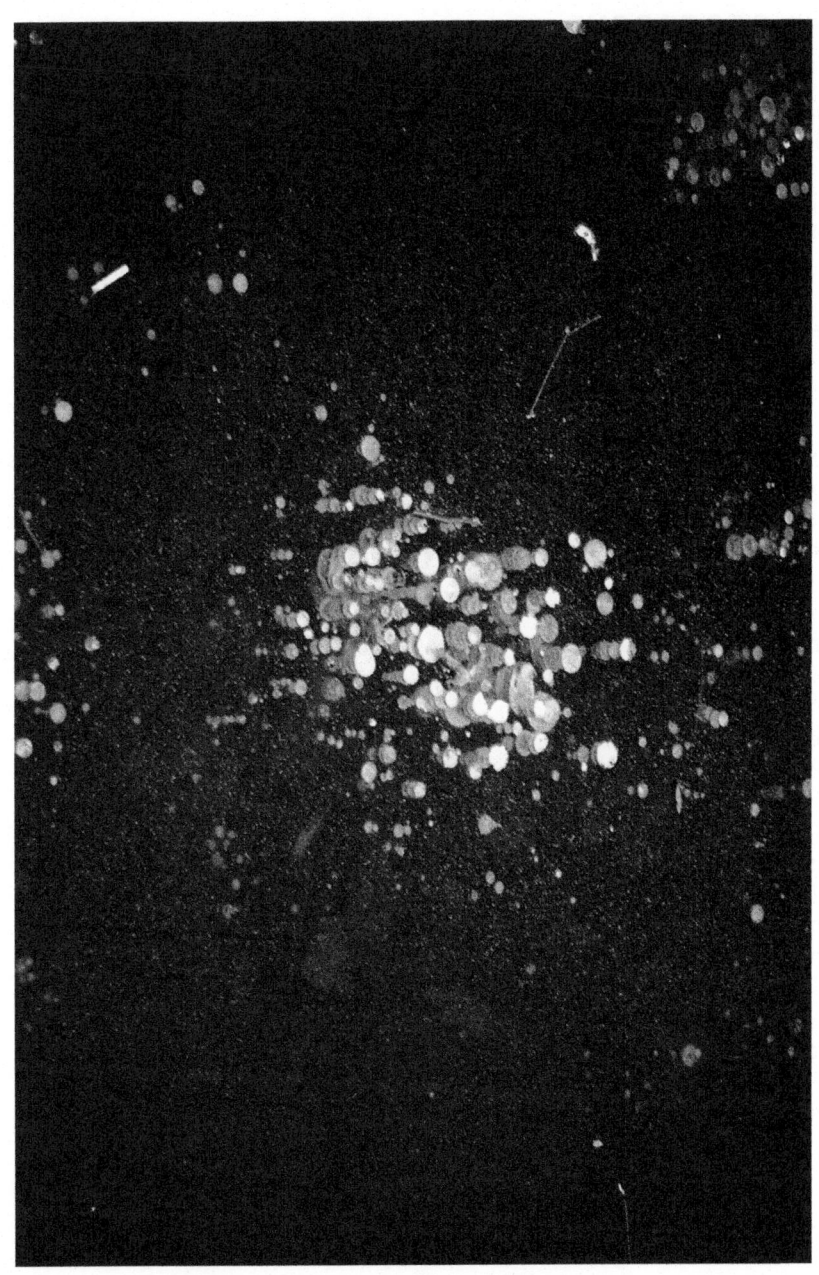

NOTHING TO BE DONE

The road into the sky that day, riverine
Pothole pocked,
              Disintegrating underfoot;
A single cat,
     As sun appeared,

Bleary, half hesitant, recalcitrant orb,
Was seen to stop,
              then dart
Away beneath a bracken hedge

Deer on the horizon,
Sharp outline of a hill punctuating,
Daisy chaining along the brow,
Small heads turned as one,
Living crenellations

Morning after,
              Exhaustion;

You disclose in disappearing
     A becoming

Figures in a landscape,
Haunting old tracks,
Feet tracing well-worn memories,
Remembrances
              Things lost.
                  Then found
Only to be abandoned.

Nothing to be done, nothing to recover

APPROPRIATION

Freud did not, could not, quite disbelieve in telepathy, for all that the scientist in him desired to disprove the possibility. Like déja vu, or the uncanny, there are moments when… But still … and yet…. So it is with the phenomena of the world in which we invest significance; or illegitimately commingling older belief systems with a modern longing, haunted by the absence of any metaphysics, for which we lack the rigour, so we hybridise with a need, but without thought; we bastardise and, in doing so, commit acts of thoughtless colonialisation, piracy in the name of a selfish desire to make ourselves more important, a narcissistic game of self-reflection that masks in its relentless self-ness the paucity of our abilities to make different the world in which we are held hostage; we co-opt and appropriate sign systems that were never ours. Anything to give meaninglessness significance.

Old roads, dirt tracks, ancestral pathways, ley lines; yew trees, wych elms, wells, and stone circles, standing stones: nothing is immune to pillage and to plunder when the spirit is at stake. For what? For the consolation of a too easy manifestation of something greater than our insignificance, as we remain, all of us, survivors on remand. The world remains before us phenomenally; we are in this, connected intimately, and still we search for something other than the very thing that is right before our noses, and to which we, in the thought of this existence, are impossibly connected.

GOOD FRIDAY

The visitors
Hesitant and bundled
Arriving at the turning point
Of a Baltic winter
Lasting until Good Friday,
Waited unequivocally.

As naked as the damned
In that brief intermission:
Fleeting instance of
A ruthless gesture, uncovering
A soul deprived of grace.

I found I was again, as for a
First, an only time, caught
Unexpecting and awry,
With neither shame, nor guilt,
Waiting in the sure and certain hope,
Of that shared, glorious identity,
Two bodies becoming one.

Epiphany in the emanation
Of a scent, lobelia coloured.

In like mind, I find
My self, ebbing into you.

JIM AND SUE

At Jim and Sue's
The road to Ashey dark,
Sky looking later,
The clock giving the lie;
Thunder rolling toward
Smallbrook;

Tom,
Five and wild,
Unearthly changeling
Screeching owl mad
In the attic.

But still we poured wine,
Playing Scrabble

– That's very rock 'n' roll
A voice, unembodied,
Out of frame,
Is heard to say,
Self-mockery in the reflection.

– More, you said
That laugh encouraging
As conversation, thoughtful,
Interrupted only
By the tumbling skyshook lightning;
Inhaling, releasing,
Slow humming giddiness.

So what's the song about?
Someone had asked,
Met first with
Silence.
Then a giggle
Before that reply:
Five and a half minutes.

[continues

MOMENTS

There are those informal moments that are never staged. Numberless, without significance, the brief passages where everything is unremarkable, in being lived out, without reflection, without pause. Those who come to be involved might be gathered by chance, as on any given evening, autumn coming on for winter, storm charged and expectant with the weight of water. A squally night, everyone inside, fires lighted, food on the table, picked at, paused over, some chosen, some left.

Evenings such as this assume a rhythm all their own, becoming in the process unrepeatable. That they take on a singular condition in memory indicates their unique quality; memory makes them all, forming, as if one were to throw a clay pot, the hands shaping and directing carefully, the importance of this one time, this epochal interruption in the onward flow of the quotidian. This is what remains in the memory: that what was special was the absolutely ordinary, the very quality to be cherished for its irrelevance. Conversations desultory, a passage of play between the figures who ghost the imagination, populating the recollection. It's a pause, a hiatus, but also passage, connective tissue between the experiences of life lived publicly. The sudden, brief drawing of the curtains, the instance of an all too transient moment behind the scenes, back stage. The small world converges in what appears as a still life, *tableau vivant*, but which is simply a motion taken out of the context of a continuum, where for that one time various lives meet, interact and then hurtle apart.

This will never come again: that which, held in the memory, has the appearance of a phatic image, an affirmation of existence moving, then suspended through a time recollected as an epoch. The figures assume a position, remaining for the memory in a certain state. Thus it is to be desired, for its quiet power to affect so vitally.

Throwing pots,
Throwing glances,
Scrabbling for the rarer word,
Unspoken though understood;
Daring interchange
Suggestive and flirtatious
In full view a foreign language
In the eye.

Stop that now!
Stoned authoritarian tone,
Parody of pedant.

This weekend, Moles
Then Exeter, this,
This, if anywhere, is where
We find the meaning
Of the tune.

But still,
There is always
The grey room.

UP AT JACK'S

i.m. Steve Griffin, Tim Muncaster, Stuart Yates

What was the experience?
Moment of a laugh recalled
Remembrance of a smile
And I confided,
     And you laughed
Balloon tied around your wrist
– A confidante, with whom to whisper

There was a hallway, long,
Well-lighted
The unfocused motion of bodies
Closely pressing

Bugger I be, Nipper! I tell 'ee what…

This came back to me, again,
In a bookstore
Named for Wilkins Micawber
Somewhere off I-95
Memory penetrates
     A present unreflection
          To unstitch all self-control

More than a few years
It opens with a flashgun, certainty;
All there in the bursting,
Bulb's whiteout

Should I recite the names today?

They would, I do believe,
Be punctuated by night horns,
Klaxons from shipping lanes

Yachts on the lee tide:
Cat rig and forestay
Freeboard and gooseneck
Chock cleat and clew
Ballast and batten, our passion
Wary of sandbanks and drifting
Proem, *prooimion*, prelude
Before the song
Vorspiel
Say that long, lovingly sibilant
Rolling out the *l*s to touch
    (We did)

                                    [continues

BALLOON

There was a party. There were fireworks. A girl with a red balloon tied around her wrist. Despite the crowding of a too-small apartment, filled warmly close with too many friends, the balloon remained unharmed throughout the night. This was all the more surprising, said the girl later, as, carefully, before bed, she detached the ribbon from her wrist, the balloon still seeking escape, considering the practical joke some idiot had played.

It was a last night, a celebration, annual, the second week of August, but always anticipated, a climax to a week on the water. The fireworks were their own highly entertaining moment. People who cared nothing for yachts loved the fireworks nonetheless. The girl had heard of them. She knew about the week, about the climax. Her friend had never been on the water, but liked fireworks also.

A girl with a red balloon. With hair as yellow as the small flowers on the always, and everywhere present, gorse bushes, *Ulex europaeus* their Latin name. Thomas Hardy insists on them, on the ubiquity of furze in The Return of the Native, their ubiquity on Egdon Heath remarkable. Literally.

So, yellow flowers, golden hair, orange car, red balloon, colours of day into night, some appearing disappearing, fireworks of memory, bursting, brightening and fading to the after image. That's memory for you. But then, in the middle of it all, yet somehow not quite remembered directly, only in the telling, and retelling of the tale, something broke into a dangerous life, white hot, glare, yellow, orange, and red. Some joker with the flare, set off in-doors, burning, smelling, making noise, and causing shouts and screams, panic in an enclosed space, the windows open, shouting the first to flee, followed by the friend of the girl with the red balloon, who climbed onto the window ledge, two floors up, believing all would turn to an incendiary madness.

No though. A passer-by, by chance another friend, at that very moment, imagine? Such a chance, what felicity.

What, said the girl with the red balloon, much later, the following morning – the balloon still hovered at the apex of her very orange tent –, what are the chances? How do you calculate this? Is it even imaginable? What are the statistics for felicity? And why would happy coincidences, in which no one believes, have another girl's name?

For the same reason, came the reply that someone, whose first and last names could equally be one half a branded appliance become Morphy rather than Hobbs, should appear. At that very instant. You couldn't make it up. It's the way these things happen.

The girl with the red balloon would not admit this. After all, he, instead of someone else, had been passing, at just that moment, in the same time, though not there for the same reason at all. Unless, it was proposed, he had come to see someone else and the fireworks. Two birds. One stone. Everybody must get lapidated.

[continues

– A very little private foreplay on the tongue
In full view, but unobserved

Oooh, fireworks!
Over the harbour to climax

Such a poem there
In the recitation of the proper name
A secret
Giving the tone
        Stimmung
            Stimmung
                Stimmung

There was a telling too,
A confession from the heart
Whispered
In the middle of a crowded room
Wood-panelled
Everything poured out,
Whisky warmed, encouraged
In the kernel;
Kate smiling indulgently,
Listening

And afterwards, she told me:
He was soooo pissed,
(That laugh, yes, that laugh
Recognition: complicity in sound)
Not a word made sense

Such dedication: this one's for you
She said, soon after,
Feeding him the bitter end,
Playing out the line

Play the chord,
She urged,
While the world falls apart

In girum imus nocte et consumimur igni

Not knowing who was in the upstairs apartment, but seeing something threatening, as yet unknown, a tall woman standing on a window ledge and a far too bright flaring glow from the room behind the open window, in he ran. Up the stairs, turning the corner. Seeing the flare, already the smell of carpet burning – how had it not caught fire? – he picked it up, throwing it into the kitchen sink. *Well bowled, sir!* Came a voice, under some influence.

It was, reflected the girl with the red balloon, a good job the sink was there. Mr Appliance could turn on the tap, extinguishing the flare, and soaking his slightly burned palm in the process.

The least I could do, she said, *was to offer him a lift home.*

SUB ROSA

Retain the secret, restrain the day's appearance;
To the world, no tell-tale sign, just that presentation
Of a private self made momentarily public.
Not for everyone, not for this one or that,
Not for the counter clerk at the corner shop,
The real, the true, the self that's only known
To very few; the motion, sure footed through the park
Belies another, the other that you carry with you,
Underneath your skin, willingly, with the care
Attendant on an unborn child, or thought made manifest
On the silence of paper, where the nakedness
Becomes tattooed, betrayed in a gesture of fidelity.
Leading, over and across, making an irreversible line,
Sense for sense, breath for breath, though staying
All the while, the fine grain, sifted apart,
Sub rosa, in camera, a recondite, impenetrable
Memory of Sanskrit in the smile's confession
Which would as likely say nothing, next to nothing,
Save for the passing smile, which
Having come to pass, takes leave,
While giving leave at dusk, to undo the day's
Impediment and check.

PROSERPINA SLEEPS

Proserpina sleeps,
Too long beneath the soil,
Abducted for her beauty,
Hidden from uncertain winds,
Feasting on pomegranates.
Sweet song Proserpina sings,
Embroidering the while
The copulation of chthonic elements,
Within dark passages;
Ordering with light and fire,
Chaos and first principles
Of things that sprang apart,
Were borne aloft, or falling
At the tapestry's farthest edge
Proserpina wakes,
Stirring, to return,
Easing the leaden season,
Eternal winter's horror fails
Swelling billows, seeds,
Drupes ripening to announce
In raised threadwork
The opening of eyes,
From bleary Night's
Bone-fingered grasp.

KHORA

The rain has not transpired; the wind causes the sky to look both ashen and leaden; it holds the weight of expectancy, as if something is immanent, just below or behind its burdened sufficiency; it is too uniform to be described as 'lowering' but has the air of a professional mourner, paid by the hour to attend the cortège. The air is charged, negative, pregnant with the appearance, semblance of a disappointment unrevealed and unrelieved. Waves appear higher than the land, as even the horizon gives the sense of upheaval, a lumpen soup of sullen resentment. At the horizon, metallic slivers appear: hinges between sea and sky. Looking down, a passing hiker might have observed the dullness of the grass, grown tired in its exposure to salt air. Looking up, the same walker would have noticed how the clouds offered a counterpoint to the grass. Sea reflects light unevenly. The front, heading east, hugging the bay. Beyond the windows, the early afternoon sky seems more October than April, more Halloween than Easter. All Souls' eve come early, world

Proserpina, was originally, in Greek polytheism, called Persephone; the daughter of Zeus and Demeter (called Jupiter and Ceres in Roman mythology), she is abducted by Hades, becoming queen of the underworld; both a chthonic and fertility goddess. Her chthonic identity is amongst the oldest of divinities, known also as Kore or Cora ('maiden'), and associated by the Romans with Libera, a native fertility goddess. Persephone, along with Demeter, goddess of harvest, was celebrated at the festival of Thesmorphia, the name deriving from the laws by which the land is worked. As figures of fertility and rebirth, the two deities, mother and daughter, may be read as belonging to a chthonic trinity, the third 'part' not an anthropomorphised figure but fertility and rebirth itself, thus inescapably belonging to cycles of life and death, the mother understood also as θεσμός (divine order and unwritten law) or Thesmorphos (bringer or bearer of that law).

The triadic condition, read by Carl Jung as Kore-Demeter-Hecate (maiden, mother, wise woman) prefigures Julia Kristeva's psychoanalytic determination of female subjectivity, the 'subject-in-process', which, in turn, is read by Kristeva in the Greek figure of *chora* or *khora*, a singularly rhythmic and amorphous feminine space. Impossible to define as such, *khora* is referred to by Heidegger as 'clearing', in and through which Being takes place and has place. Described by Derrida as neither sensible nor intelligible as such, *khora* neither has place nor is place, yet, as radical otherness, gives place to the generation of meaning. *Khora* is defined by John Caputo thus: "neither present nor absent, active or passive, the good nor evil, living nor nonliving – but rather atheological and nonhuman – khôra is not even a receptacle. Khôra has no meaning or essence, no identity to fall back upon. She/it receives all without becoming anything, which is why she/it can become the subject of neither a philosopheme nor mytheme. In short, the khôra is tout autre [fully other], very."

and time unhinged, seasons and solstices confused, life submerged. Welter and wreak, cloud shards rent, wrack hurled into a sky overturned and mocking the water below. Here is Hallowmas, untimely driven, wind rending the trees, the bushes, and plants; azaleas molested, petals destroyed, rose buds wrenched from thorny stems, thrown profligate about, as if, lately, the house has been abandoned in a hurry. Day is turning a midnight grey, the detail of the visible world erased. Wind heaves and sighs. A wordless voice, last breathing heave. And then: no more. Come to dust. Sky shows little light: a dour sun, weak, enfeebled, muffled, smothered in the rags of tattered cloud blanket pressing onward. The weight of a bruise. Image of whatever aches in you. Everything stalled.

STIMMUNGSTRÄGER

There you are.

We were caught, one time,
Distant to the world
Though so close to one another,
Drifting, *dérive, dérive – on y va!*
Draping ourselves, each in the other, invisibly clothed

Dream, you said,
The air shapes winter's depth,
A Devil's bargain –
    There was a word, you said,
        For sure, a word that captured everything
Though Flemish, unforgiving in the mouth

Eden red the sky that morning
In the secret garden
Hidden away. Swinburne could never guess
But only fake,
So flawed the human heart
Captured in a Japanese garden.

Listening to the meshworks
Of passing conversation, as we,
Hidden, laughed laughingly in the silence
In the midst of
Moments of negotiation
Leaving the path, lips dry
The tongue to stick
A Parched kiss –
    Partir – Parterre!
I drift in silent music, was all your confession
As, sky high,
A desert hum consumed espaliered fruits

To lick, in sticky sweetness all condemned
And caught, captured, as a tape warp
Oscillation of the 'cello's throat
Commingling with Ventnor bells,
Was thought to be heard,
                      (– *But how?*)

[continues

BIRD TRAPS AND LIGHTHOUSES

STIMMUNGSTRÄGER

Da bist du.

Wir waren gefangen, einmal,
Fern der Welt
Doch so nah beieinander,
Driftend, *dérive, dérive – on y va!*
Uns umhüllend, einer im Anderen, unsichtbar bekleidet

Träume! sagtest Du,
Die Luft formt des Winters Tiefe,
Ein Handel mit dem Teufel –
     Es gäbe ein Wort, sagtest Du,
     Sicherlich, ein Wort, das alles erfasse.
Wenn auch Flämisch, unversöhnlich im Mund

Edenrot der Himmel an jenem Morgen
Im dem geheimen Garten
Verborgen. Swinburne konnte niemals erraten
Sondern nur vortäuschen,
So unvollkommen das menschliche Herz
Gefangen in einem Japanischen Garten.

Zuhörend dem Geflecht
Eines flüchtigen Gesprächs, als wir,
Versteckt, lachend lachten in der Stille
Inmitten von
Momenten der Verhandlung
Den Weg verlassend, Lippen trocken,
die Zunge bleibt kleben,
Ein trockener Kuss –
     Partir – Parterre!
Ich drifte in stiller Musik, war dein einziges Bekenntnis
Wie, himmelhoch,
Ein verlassenes Summen Früchte am Spalier verzehrte

Zu lecken, ganz in klebriger Süße verdammt

Und gefangen, gefasst, wie ein Bandwurm
Eine Schwingung des 'Cello Halses
Sich vermischend mit Ventnor Glocken
Glaubte man zu hören,
                  (– *Doch wie?*)

Sometimes, just sometimes, more often than we care to admit, there remains the all too untranslatable. A residue that cannot be rendered into a statement. Remaining immovable, even before translation, from one tongue to another, before any transposition from what we might conventionally describe as its original tongue, a word bears within itself so much more than can be put into words. There is everything – and all the rest. In this manner, a word serves as a prompt to excessive and unbidden overflow, much like a memory, that instant of bright recollection, on a frost bright day, cold and hard.

Without the possibility of expectation, we find ourselves caught, halted, paused in the blink of an eye, captured like birds in the traps of one of Breughel's medieval hunters by what might it be called a resonance. The word *Stimmungsträger* arrived thus, unexpectedly, one February morning. A sign in a gallery, a temporary display showing works from the permanent collection of a museum, the *Kunsthalle Hamburg*, undergoing refurbishment. This one word, printed large, given a prominence announcing that one was entering onto choices intended to exemplify the significance of the word itself, called me to a halt.

[continues

Bare beneath Boniface, revealed,
Delirious pulchritude undressed that morning.

(I can see from your eyes how much you loved the strange word for the obvious)

– *You don't say!*

And after all, she was heard to whisper,
Tomorrow is another day.

Nackt unterhalb des Bonifatius, offenbart,
Wahnsinnige Schönheit entkleidet an jenem Morgen.

(Ich kann an deinen Augen sehen wie sehr du das seltsame
Wort für das Offensichtliche liebtest)

– *Was du nicht sagst!*

Und schließlich, konnte man sie flüstern hören,
ist Morgen ein neuer Tag.

The word was unknown to me. I recognised *Stimmung*: a noun signifying mood, feeling, tone, tenor, tuning (of an instrument). My *Duden* puts it this way, regarding one definition: *das Gestimmtsein eines Instruments*. *Gestimmt*: in tune, tempered, but also, in a phrase such as mild-mannered: *freundlich gestimmt*. And *Sein*, to be or to constitute, considered as verb, Being, when spelt with a capital S, or existence. So, the being of a manner or temper, the tone's being of an instrument. This is, though, only one of two entries under the subheading *Musik*.

The adjective – also untranslatable – is used in the first definition, to indicate something that is revealed almost instantaneously, the appearance having about it the quality of being in the blink of an eye, 'blink-of-an-eye-ness', might be the quality of the experience, were English capable of moving wholesale the weight of significance. *Träger*, on the other hand, a girder, a beam, a carrier, a bearer, the means, a repository, a supporter, the support of a function. *Stimmungsträger* then: the bearing or disposition of the mood and atmosphere, that which carries the tone, the substrate, of mood, tone, pitch, atmosphere; or *Stimmungsbild*, an atmospheric picture.

All of which is, or was, mere preface to another morning, the same week. The image of birds in lime, analogous to a photograph, a snapshot in memory, which bore with its recollection a snowy morning walking past the nearly frozen lake, arrived suddenly to arrest progress, bringing with it, being the bearer of the mood, the tone, an atmosphere complementary to ice cold grey sky day. Mood within mood, image and phrase alike resonating with the tintinnabulation of the heart's perfectly attuned resonance. A now, and then, another now, the word having arrived to provide the vessel and determination, though untranslatable, for the arrival of the scene, in which the trace of memory appeared, and, all at once, self-contained, contained within the container, and yet, overflowing the limits of each instant, the one within, giving way to another, and another, unfurling from within, even as further and further back the recession went, spilling out, and across time, to fill the present and give pause. All to end in the recollection of another's words, returning, trace of a different story, a fiction from the 1920s of all things; which words – *tomorrow is another day* – bring the as yet unfulfilled promise of the arrival and, with that, a new tone, to supplement, replace, overwrite, the disappointment of the present.

So, buy me a thought. I'll tell you the way I feel.

But I won't tell you everything, not because I couldn't, but because there are some things that refuse to be put into words. There are others that should never be told. And there are those, in between, all around, which have never had words to stand in for the otherwise unspoken experience.

CORVID (for Andrew)

The magpie walks.
Nothing to imagine, it picks at nothing.
One step, two steps, three steps, four –
It does not, cannot count,
Its idle progress in the damping air,
Just the motion of
Gathering life.

Up the steps
Down the steps,
An errand without definition – I
Would tell you that
The magpie broke its journey;
Everything, you say,
Breaks off its journey,
Whether or no the intention was there

We see eye to eye
In the half closed door we find
Another direction.
Water shines: this winter morning.

Break off,
Turn the sod,
Bruts and chits, they're not the same.
For many, they have no existence
Because irrelevant.

The ignorance of the without why
Their only defence, a gambit,
Less a strategy not to know
Not to want to know,
Not knowing not to want not –

But, knowing that, you told me all the secrets
In a last and lingering look
As the magpie turns,
Descending interrupted
Time idles it seems,
In the ground under our feet

On the boards of an empty room, you lay.

La rose est sans pourquoi

THE UNDECIDABLE

In a comment on Hélène Cixous' *Manhattan*, Jacques Derrida points out that what we are told in that narrative happened in reality; it is not *just* a fiction, however fictionally rendered. However, such is the law of the literary that it is impossible to decide whether this 'in reality' – in our case, the tale the poem presents – hides a further simulacrum; whether it marks the beginning of one more fiction.

You observe one day, as you walk to work, a bird. Birds fly. From a human perspective, this is their nature. Flying, the idea of flight, is part of how we define the purpose, the meaning of the bird. Not content with giving something a name, we have to give it purpose or meaning. Not content with giving the 'bird' a name, we have to offer some significance for that name, as though name, motion and meaning were all intrinsically interwoven.

The bird does not know this; does not know it's a bird. It has no sense, whatever sense it may have, of its own birdness. It exists in itself without this self-distancing awareness. So, it strikes you as remarkable – worthy of comment – that the bird appears, for no other reason that you can discern, to walk a flight of steps. It is in the absence of reason that some other reason appears to lie. The absence may not be, for you or me, an absence at all, but instead, an enigma, a wonder pertaining to a mystery, lying at the heart of the incomprehensibility, from a merely human perspective, of this act. Whether or not the bird has a reason is irrelevant. The relevance is in our ability to fail to let be, but at the same time, to pause over the undecidable that resides at the very division between comprehensibility and incomprehensibility. That we do not understand; that we fail to invent significance, but remain in the face of the undecidable, never knowing whether there is significance; and if there is, whether it resides beyond all calculation or discernibility: such dwelling is without question, our ownmost possibility. Angelus Silesius was correct. The rose is without why.

CORVID (pour Andrew)
La pie se promène.
Rien à imaginer, elle picore en vain.
Un pas, deux pas, trois pas, quatre –
Elle ne sait pas, ne peut pas compter,
Son parcours sans but dans l'air humide,
Juste l'apparence
De glaner la vie.

Elle monte les marches
Elle descend les marches,
Une course sans sens – Je
Vous raconterais que
Son voyage prit fin;
Tout, dites-vous,
Prend fin,
Qu'on le veuille ou non.

Nous voyons, ensemble
Par la porte entreouverte
Une autre direction.
L'eau scintille: ce matin d'hiver.

En finir,
Retourner la motte de terre,
Drageons et pousses, ils ne sont pas équivalents.
Pour beaucoup, ils n'ont aucune existence
Car ils importent peu.

L'ignorance du sans pourquoi
Leur unique défense, une tactique,
Moins une stratégie pour ne pas savoir
Ne pas vouloir savoir,
Ne pas savoir ne pas vouloir pas –

Mais, sachant cela, tu m'as raconté tous les secrets
En un dernier regard qui s'attarde
Comme la pie tourne,
Descente interrompue
Le temps semble tourner au ralenti,
Dans la terre sous nos pieds

Sur les planches d'une sale vide tu étais allongée.
Die Ros ist ohne warum

SONG

I'm giving up on fffffssss
We need less Ks,
Too many though I have
Already memory stored
The sound repeating, false Corvid call
Tape loop signalling the past
At regular intervals,
As if an ever-present opening
Hoping for a future different
(Experience tells us otherwise);
They come,
The return, revenance in sound
To inspire the image hovering;
Yes, Ks we have,
    (And just one M to last a lifetime)
Far fewer ls –

        X

        An irrelevance mistaken for a mystery
In plain sight.

M hovers
    Mmmmmmmm

    A private song along the wires, wireless, in and all around
        Finding its flight within air's roiling turbulence

Arriving safely, to alight, mouth on mouth, tongue on tongue
Conjoined, conjoining, *donnant donnant*

The dunnock without the window sings
Insistent in the morning, fresh and fast,
Heart calling greets the spring
A voice not given to hesitation
Joined by warbler and pipit.

ARBITRARY

The whimsical, the random, the chance, and erratic, all have their part to play. Whether or not they are truly groundless, unmotivated, discretional; these are all other matters. So used to the idea of order, craving it without realising this, we confer on the alphabet a greater power than it has. But were you to free the letters from the words that spring most readily to mind – what do you think of if I say or write this or that letter? What word, what noun or pronoun appears before you? Does the letter conjure a face, a person, a memory of such, the letter mere siglum signalling so much more than the apparent diminution of its cryptic shape?

With every letter, at every instant of the figure refigured, troped this way or that, there is, in whatever difference the letter makes, a future, as yet unprescribed, not even pre-scribed, not yet written ahead of the 'initial' inscription. And there is a past, many pasts, for as many uses, appearances, momentary utterances. You cannot hope to trace back every use, the very dream of which admits an abyssal and therefore hopeless, fruitless desire. The future? Give it up, whatever comes will come when it does, giving and taking, a shuttle on a loom, making connections in the instant of the motion's passage, coming to pass and returning. That returning is always already written into the inscription, a palimpsest ghosted onto and within, a shadow tattoo, ghost-guest of the shape in other tongues and words as yet unspoken, indeed, never spoken, for, ask yourself: how can something be unspoken, strictly speaking?

In anticipating what cannot be anticipated you already speak ahead of speaking. Your anticipation is itself the spoken, the inscribed.

ULYSSES ON A NORTHERN SHORE

Ulysses on a northern shore –
A smaller craft, bare wooden boards,
Though painted red, no sail, no mast,
Two oars, with no direction, save the heart
From which to guide, with which to steer –
Landed at this eastern strand in colder waters, silvered skies,
Sand grey in twilight's fall,
Though off, an horizontal line
White gold, Ionian in memory
Refracted in this, Atlantic sibling.

Guided north, magnetic was the tow,
Unlooked for, though directed without will;
Through Skaggerak, through Kattegat,
Navigating islands, working blind
Past Bornholm-memory in the inner ear
As if a farther echo, Echo's call, never Penelope's
Sound of the sea, deep within a shell,
To land thus, momently confused,
On finding olive trees, the pits spat scattered.
Food for roosting crows, ash, lilac, jasmine, privet too recalled,
Olea europaea, the diasporic family.

Last gleam, shell catching, cylinder,
Bright coloured gastropod,
A home without inhabitant.
No turning home, no return, only here
For the homeless sailor, the wanderer
Who, everywhere sees nothing,
Though in that nothing sees the very absence
For which he longs, a fleeting figure once encountered
At the height of summer, solstice not long past.

So, taken by the tides, trusting to the heart's clews,
He finds he has arrived.
A sigh, a tear, and looking down
To clear his eyes, a shadow falls across his weariness,
The silhouette of the beloved stands in the setting sun.
Here, she seems to say, is home, though voiceless and unmoving;
Here, your harbour, here your refuge, here a place to cradle your desires.

A DAY

A day.
A fine day;
Another fine day;
This is always the memory
In the moment that I step into the same place

Time after time
Place become time becoming

I enter this field,
There, the sea,
(I feel invisibly the pressure of an exclamation)
Southernmost,
As the place, present, past,
Folds itself around me
With the ghost of your body
Close behind
By surprise
(Everything assumes its place by stealth,
As if we wore parentheses around our smiles)

The lighthouse
It remains
As it was,
As it is, and as it shall remain.

I wait
Waiting
Waiting for the wind
Waiting for the wind to change,
I scent
I scent the shift,
Turn and turn around,
Sensing nothing but
The slowly widening circle

It is so simple,
So very easy,
Just let go, letting go,
Turning into the downward flow
A current catches as a breath.

[continues

RECLAMATION

UNE JOURNÉE

Une journée
Une belle journée
Encore une belle journée
Ca c'est toujours la mémoire
Au moment de me mettre dans le même endroit

A maintes reprises sans cesse
L'endroit devient le temps devenant

J'entre dans ce pré
Là, la mer
(Je me sens invisiblement la pression d'une exclamation).
A l'extrême sud
Comme l'endroit, présent, passé
M'emballe dans ses plis
Avec le fantôme de ton corps
De près derrière
Au dépourvu
(Tout adopte sa place furtivement
Les sourires rayonnants guirlandés de parenthèses).

La phare
Elle reste
Comme elle était
Comme elle reste, et comme elle restera.

J'attends
L'attente
Attendant que le vent tourne
Je sens
Je sens le changement
Tourne et se retourne
Sentant rien sauf
Le cercle lentement élargissant.

C'est si facile
Enormément facile
Tout simplement, laisser aller, laissant aller,
Se fondant dans l'écoulement descendant
Un courant attrape comme le dernier souffle.

Language claims us.

Language reclaims us.

Before the subject, before you and I, before we arrive, to reflect, to name, to speak of what we see, and how we understand and receive the world; and before we reconstruct the worlds we have inhabited, there, *there*, in a place of its own, is language. We enter the world as we enter into the words we apply, employ, and wield, to speak in and of this or that world.

Language does not wait for us to speak it. It makes us its subjects, giving us, there in its non-present presence (for there is no *there* as such, there is no material existence to language, it is not some thing, to be grasped or handled) a constellated gathering of arbitrary signs. It claims us, it calls out to us, and, becoming human, we respond.

This is the law of the human subject, the law, the law and rule of language, before which all human beings stand, subject to its utterances, and only able to communicate, if at all, in those signs, according to the laws by which language engages the subject as its advocate.

Clamare (verb): to call out

Language claims us. Language calls us. Language calls to us, calls out to us. To realise our Being, we are obligated to respond. Response to the call, responding to the call, responding as a correspondent within the language of the call: this is our responsibility. To be claimed is to be called. Call and response. This is who we are.

But we are also reclaimed by language. Language reclaims us. It recollects, recalls us, bringing us back to ourselves, I to you, you to me. The ones who are lost are never truly gone because they return in our response to that call.

[continues

I watch the gull describe
A dying arc
Comforting air
Buoyant with summer's promise

You fly
Without effort,
Without wings
– Unless you have grown them
Since we were last here.

Quite possible.

And so, yes, I hear that coming
Once more, you lovingly mimic
A voice,
My own I do believe.

And there it is, the lighthouse.
Tomorrow, you had said,
Will be another,
A day
Another day,
Another fine day

Fine

To turn the soil,
Turning out the ground

Appearing to memory, they become reclaimed, recollected, remembered, and we find ourselves in the midst of an ethical responsibility, to bear witness, to attest, to speak of the dead, to speak in their place, when their place no longer exists as such.

We may, some of us, perhaps, seek through our response, our responsible recollection, to reclaim through language's power of reclamation, the trace of each and every other. This is of course no more than a hypothesis, not an affirmation of fact.

Every word is a trace, each trace a re-presentation of the other, as well as the other's re-presentation: the former, the trace, is a return; it is a revenant that presents that which is no longer present as such or available. The latter, the re-presentation (a term Husserl uses, distinct from 'representation'), is the psychic and phenomenological imago, the image of that return, that reclamation.

So as we stake our claim, calling out to the other, seeking in that calling to respond and recollect, in order that we may reclaim what we can, language, so many shells, so much bracken on the shoreline, washed up by the tide; so much shale, sand, shingle, that will hold between the jaws of some mechanical scooper, while the sea drains away between the teeth.

Language reclaims us.

Language claims us.

Je vois la mouette qui décrit
Un arc mourant
L'air apaisant
Flottante avec la promesse de l'été.

Tu voles
Sans effort
Sans ailes
– A moins que t'en aies laisser pousser
Depuis notre dernier rendezvous ici.

Tout à fait possible

Et oui, je l'ai entendu venir
Encore une fois, tu imites tendrement
Un voix.
La mienne, je le crois bien.

Et la voilà, la phare
Demain, tu l'avais dit,
Sera une autre
Une journée
Encore une journée
Encore une belle journée.

Bien.

Tourner la terre
Sillonant le sol.

DRAPING THE SKY FOR A SNOWFALL (LÜBECK)

Greycast, seagull stirred
Leaden portents mining
In day defying light
Weighting expectation,
Great the pause

Of all before the coming
Of Night's dusting welcome
Building unlifted,
Unbuilding upsprung geometries
Sky caesura pocked
    Those shades
    Pretending
    Each to the other
    Unnoticeable

Glück ist, wenn die Katastrophe eine Pause macht

The duck skates poorly
If at all, land-sliding
To eventful halt, faulting
On ice
Barfuß is the word: barefoot webfoot
Landingly
The graceless motion anticipating
The thought of *Schadenfreude*

    – *Nos videntium te*

Stimmungsträger

Reflections of a mood in Being's Time
Encouraged, nurtured, engendered
Between
        Zwischen
Two languages, tongue shuttling,
My mouth, yours, the warm moment in the cold
Shuttle weave, the bobbin instant
Of a memory – *Traumwerk* – of *Heimat*
For which I cannot frame a word,
Refracted through that hopefulness, yes
Sehnsucht

        [continues

DEN HIMMEL FÜR EINEN SCHNEEFALL EINHÜLLEN (LÜBECK)

Graubedeckt, von Möwen aufgerührt
Bleierne Vorzeichen graben
Im Licht, das dem Tage trotzt,
Erwartung beschwerend,
Groß die Pause

Von Allem bevor dem Kommen
Des bestäubenden Willkommens der Nacht
Bauend ungehoben
Emporgeschossene Geometrien abbauend
Himmelszäsur pockennarbig
       Jene Schattierungen
       Vorspielend
       Einer dem Anderen
       Unbemerkbar

Glück ist, wenn die Katastrophe eine Pause macht

Die Ente ist eine schlechte Eisläuferin,
Wenn überhaupt, rutscht sie auf der Erde
Bis zu einem ereignisreichen Stillstand,
einen Fehler begehend
Auf dem Eis
Barfuß ist das Wort: Barfußnetzfuß
Auf landenden Weise
Die unelegante Bewegung antizipiert
Den Gedanken von Schadenfreude

    – Nos videntium te

Stimmungsträger

Betrachtungen einer Stimmung in der Zeit
des Daseins
Ermuntert, gehegt, erzeugt
Zwischen
      Zwischen
Zwei Sprachen, die Zunge pendelnd,
Mein Mund, Deiner, der warme Moment in
der Kälte
Pendeln weben, der Klöppel Augenblick
Einer Erinnerung – Traumwerk – der Heimat
Für die ich kein Wort formen kann,
Gebrochen durch dieses hoffnungsvolle Gefühl, ja
Sehnsucht

Walking through the day, he gathered, to himself, the smallest signs on a winter's morning. The nightworld had taken brief hold, with white, with ice, with the shading of the sky becoming heavy in light. It is as if he thought to himself, watching the ducks land awkwardly, this small world were assuming a significance for a mood yet to emerge, fully.

How strange, the language of an advertisement for a chocolate bar, when seen from outside that tongue, one that, though familiar, is nevertheless not one's own. As though a language were the possession of someone, rather than every person being in the possession of language.

Standing at the half-frozen edge, he watched a while, camera to hand, fingers growing colder, losing all sense of time in watching the various water fowl, in the comic negotiation of a nearly alien medium.

The everyday, unreflected, is, all the while and at the same time, a pause waiting to happen, a moment pregnant with the possibility of philosophical reflection. The opportunity is there to think existence.

If one wishes; or as the chance gives itself to one.

[continues

There it is, you knew,
Didn't you?

You knew it would arrive
And Caspar still stands,
The Man on the mountain, back turned out to the world
Looking into the vanishing point

What does he feel?
What perspective his?

We stand behind him, never knowing

The rain came late with the memory of you
Sky darkening – darkling a word, yes – as tea was served
Ginger tasting, lemon at first
    In Kiel
Schrecklich was the word, another, gather them
    Schlechtwetter
        Schrecklich
            Sch, sch, sch, sch, sch
Rain glass running on a Friday afternoon,
The smell of chalk in the classroom
Another Caspar, no not Friedrich
        Friedrich Freitag, you laughed
Giggling, the five-year-old she comes
To step away
        (pli selon pli)
Glass swept rain, finger dragging
Scraping chalkboard. *Endlos*
    (Heard in corridors)

        And you tell me nothing

Eiskalt, Arschkalt

Small world frosted white
Sabine speaks my name
As leaves grow fur-rime, dry prickle,
Rhumb, rheum turned to that
Imaginary line, frozen in place
All meridians the same,
Any of the 32 points, now

A leaf in imitation of a kiwi
Eisendorf, iron village dressed in ice, waits asleep
So much white that Sunday morning
So much, that darker shapes turn silhouette in sympathy

[continues

Da ist es, Du wusstest es,
Nicht wahr?

Du wusstest, dass es kommen würde
Und Caspar steht immer noch,
Der Mann auf dem Berg, mit dem Rücken (hinaus) zur Welt gedreht
In den Fluchtpunkt hineinschauend

Was fühlt er?
Was seine Perspektive?

Wir stehen hinter ihm, nie wissend

Der Regen kam spät mit der Erinnerung an Dich
Der Himmel verdunkelt sich – ein düsteres
Wort, ja – als Tee serviert wurde
Nach Ingwer schmeckend, Zitrone zuerst
    In Kiel
Schrecklich war das Wort, noch eins, sammle Sie
    Schlechtwetter
        Schrecklich
            Sch, sch, sch, sch, sch
Regen Glas laufen an einem Freitag Nachmittag,
Der Geruch von Kreide im Klassenzimmer
Ein anderer Caspar, nein nicht Friedrich
    Friedrich Freitag, lachtest Du
Kichernd, die Fünf-Jährige, sie kommt
Um wegzutreten
    (pli selon pli)
Vom Glas gewischter Regen, Finger schleifen
Kratzen die Tafel. Endlos
    (In Fluren überhört)

    Und Du erzählst mir nichts

Eiskalt, Arschkalt

Kleine Welt, weiß von Frost
Sabine sagt meinen Namen
Als aus Blättern Raureif wächst, trocken stachln,
Rhumb, Rheum verwandelt in jene
Imaginäre Linie, erstarrt an Ort und Stelle
Alle Meridiane gleich
Alle der 32 Punkte, nun

Ein Blatt in Nachahmung einer Kiwi
Eisendorf, Eisen-Dorf in Eis gekleidet, wartet schlafend
So viel Weiß an jenem Sonntag Morgen
So viel, dass dunklere Formen sich in Silhoutten verwandeln aus Mitleid

    [continues

It would be as if, he thought, he were able to stand, outside himself, like that man on the mountain, and able to look at his other self, the one who looks, but is unaware of being watched. And so, he reflected, the first, that one whose back is seen, might never be aware of being watched. Though equally, he may have come, at another instant, in another location, a different time, to a not dissimilar conclusion. The reflection opens itself, with a potentially dizzying endlessness.

Pausing to watch, memory opens, in the stasis. It's all there, the taste of a tea. Proust had been right all along. And from there, from the sky's shade, the rest arrives. In the memory, inside the returning image, another. Image upon image, Matryoshka: each memory the mother, the vessel, of the next, and the preceding one. Endless, one inside the other, one leading to the other. So many traces, visual echoes. Here and there. Then and now, and then again, though differently. But still, no confirmation, the speculation unresolved.

Yet one more memory, a walk in the snow, another occasion, an old friend, the urge to share secrets. Why should this, now, appear, he wondered, without answer. But still, there was the voice, itself unanswered.

For the silence of a day submerged
Dusted
A thin fog drifts
Visibly and slow,
The snow falls quick upon the lake,
Larger, smaller
    By the *Brahmsee* where we walked
    Wardersee adjacent

And you said
Jan, he was so very angry,
But that was my father, how could I?

Slow, crow motion
Crackle, *knurren*, gnaw, *die Hunde knurren*

Unterschiedlos,
    Unterschiede Körpersprache
        Märchenstunde
            Knurren ist mangelnder Respekt

At the edge of the village, stands a man
The stepfather in outline
This image pushes forward, toward me
In the creeping, breathing air
As we sit in half light,
Tea light,
Kitchen warmed, *sauerkraut* scented;
The cat upon the table,
Listening to the flutter of small wings,
Then comes the crow once more,
Knurren, knurren, knurren
A laugh much like
The scratch of death
Insistent in the stillness

Still
        Silent

                Stille

The weight of a day's fragments

Für die Stille eines versunkenen Tages
Bestäubt
Ein dünner Nebel driftet
Sichtbar und langsam,
Der Schnee fällt schnell auf den See,
Größer, kleiner,
      Am Brahmsee wo wir gingen   *Impossible to know, to tell, so silence in response.*
        Wardersee nebenan

Und Du sagtest
Jan, er war so bitterböse,
Aber es war mein Vater, wie konnte ich nur?

Langsam, Krähen Bewegung   *The only sound in the midst of snowfall, the crow:*
Knistern, *knurren*, nagen, *die Hunde knurren*   *Crow voiced air, crackle, static in the winter sky.*

Unterschiedslos,
    Unterschiede Körpersprache
        Märchenstunde
           Knurren ist mangelnder Respekt

Am Rande des Dorfes steht ein Mann   *Later that day, they returned, to warm with tea,*
Der Umriss des Stiefvaters   *plum tart, and candles lighted on the kitchen table,*
Dieses Bild schiebt sich vorwärts, zu mir hin   *In the room, shadows cast on lemon yellow walls.*
In der schleichenden, atmenden Luft   *There remained that Sunday afternoon, and later,*
Als wir im Zwielicht sitzen,   *travelling over the days, that uncomfortable ghost*
Teelicht,   *of the unrepentant stepfather, hovering over all.*
Die Küche erwärmt, nach Sauerkraut duftend;
Die Katze auf dem Tisch
Lauschend dem Flattern von kleinen Flügeln,
Dann kommt die Krähe noch einmal,
Knurren, knurren, knurren,
Ein Lachen sehr ähnlich   *Now as then, in the middle of the city, as at the*
Dem Kratzer des Todes   *edge of the smaller, unliving village that winter's*
Beharrlich in der Stille   *day, crow sounding the counterpoint to a clock, a*
                                            bell tower, chimes recalling the steady tock tock
                                            tock. Insistent, yes, as were the interstices wherein
                                            everything remains, waiting to come back.

    Still
            Silent

                    Stille

Die Last der Fragmente eines Tages

NAMELESS

Arbre à fleurs
odorantes
– Tu est
un bel acacia
à fleurs blanches

White flowered wattle,
Whistling thorn,
– Mimosidae –
Leaves opening,
Closing,
To the touch.

Linnaeus
First described this,
Giving shapes in tongues
Old and new, to
Nameless growth
Along the Nile.

Slender, pliable,
With silent strength,
The sweet pea a cousin
Though lacking
ἀκίς

FORGET ME NOT

Your voice sighs
Wind in the rigging
Westerly
        Myosotis

At the harbour's edge
Where marsh and tidal
Hearts tug
Shaping the bay

Lagoon formed eddies
Slough water wrack kelp scented sour
A ballast of longing
On the wind

And

At the turning of the tide
A bell irregularly
Marks the motion
Of your unanchoring soul
As

Adrift

The steering gone
Unruddered
But felt within
The curlew song

I am the wreck of my own loss

THE MOUSE'S EAR

The mouse's ear provides a source of food for the larvae of the setaceous Hebrew character, on the forewings of which there is a dark mark, resembling nothing so much as the Hebrew letter *nun,* the fourteenth letter of several tongues, including Phoenician, Aramaic, Syriac and Arabic. From this derives the Cyrillic H and the Latin N, though the origin, hypothesised as the Egyptian hieroglyph for snake or eel, has no certain foundation. As with all origins, this is mythological in its undecidability.

The name 'mouse's ear' is a translation of *myosotis*, but this is not the name used in the vernacular. Though the plant bears the name *myosotis* (of which there are more than 70 species of the genus), its given name refers not to the flower but to the leaf. That is the forget-me-not, the name of which is not a translation but a calque, first appearing in English in 1398, a substitution for the German *Vergissmeinnicht*.

Calque is both noun and verb, also known by linguists as a 'loan translation' (which is itself a loan translation, or calque, from the German *Lehnübersetzung*). As a noun, the term refers to a word or phrase that borrows word for word, or, so to say, *verbatim*, from the language it bears over, from one tongue to another, across the lingual border. It might be said that forget-me-not is not then, to elaborate, a translation as such, which is, *in stricto sensu*, an act of conveyance. Translation thus shares its root with the idea of the transfer, itself naming the legality of the action, being bound up with property rights.

Calque is carried over untranslated, though it is, itself, not properly a calque, being a French term imported, remaining itself, the tongue transferred, transplanted, much like a species of plant uprooted from its native soil, given a new home. It is therefore that which is also known as a 'loanword' (or in German, *Lehnwort*, another example of a calque rather than a translation), and is derived in turn from the verb *calquer*, signifying the act of tracing or copying.

REPRESENTATIONS

Someone asked me
Recently
As if desirous of
Enlightenment –
    When will you abandon the past?
Never
    Was my reply
For

    I explained

The past has not abandoned me
The beloved dead are no less beloved
Though they fail in the return
Careless of all that is
Uncountable, the very thing
We want to give

They are no less beloved

Because they insist on waking us
At 2.22
Every morning
Leaving us only with the facile treasures
Of nighttime radio
All of which we will have forgotten

But no
Absence is not abandonment
The heart, being full and eloquently silent
Gives the lie to reason

THE UNCOUNTABLE

It is a question of grammar, arriving circuitously through the buried etymologies of love. Love, I am tempted to say, just is the uncountable. You cannot count on love. Neither can you measure, quantify, or economise on love. Resistant to anything having to do with rationality or ratios, love cannot be counted, it is innumerate. Even in its singularity – the love that happens to you, that takes place, that comes to pass, in the event that you recognise, or apprehend the gift of the other, happens to no one else, never again – it is only knowable in its singularity through the condition that, paradoxically it is also iterable.

Nothing as such, always coming to pass, taking place, love is singular *and* iterable, the same and not the same, the one reflected on as perceivable, as the analogous apperception of the other. For, and here is the paradox: for the singular to be apprehensible as singular, it has, in principle, to be transmissible. It cannot be absolutely singular, for otherwise it would remain unavailable as a singularity to perception. However, its 'repetition' is never a pure repetition, but rather it is iterable, which is to say its repetition bears the trace of a difference. Neither exactly the same nor completely different, the iterable trace is what bears the singularity across, translates it as such, remaining faithful, while betraying it.

And it's always taking place, between, in between.

But love, originally Sanskrit and Indo-European, distinguishable in its earliest linguistic form from desire though announced in the same form (*lubhyati*), arrives, lands on the English tongue as a Norse and Old High German immigrant, having charted a course, across, around the Baltic, written as *luve*. As a noun, love has also signified a noun that cannot be used with numbers or the indefinite article, and so takes no plural form. To insinuate a strong reading here, love just is that which is irreducible to number or measure.

To tell the other your love, what you call yours but which in fact is already, always, the affirmation of the other; to say this is to say, in effect, *I cannot measure this feeling I have for you, it is beyond calculation or measurement.*

THERE IS THIS

Everything that matters
Takes place in secret
In the twilight of a European city.
There, at a corner,
Or in some café,
A gentle hiss obscures
The finer contours of
A soft spoken conversation,
As, cobble street heeled,
A figure, retreating,
Dreams of a warmer welcome,
Early on an unclouded afternoon,
November for sure,
The third week of the month;

And there is this to be said:
Looking into the eyes
Of the only other,
A sound is felt, scraping of a bow,
A 'cello's wooden eminence,
Two notes realised as a single
Point of purpose, transcendent,
Bowing the one, the soul
Inside the thought.

SCENTED

The field below the windmill
Bears the shape of a love long absent
While, in the air,
Cecily Cardew is overheard
Whispering
To Robert Zimmerman
He reads Tennyson, unheeding
Her entreaties, and waiting
For the last bus home

A sound in the copse
Snuffling with expectations of violence
Disturbs the calm of
The light crepuscular

A change is being practised
Figures dark dressed
In black face
Leave the barn
An owl passes
The grass remains
Holding still to your body's pressure

        As if

                As if

                        As if

You had only recently

                      Left

This figure, *as if*, is an important figure or rhetorical / phenomenological trope in Jacques Derrida's writing. Taken in part from the Kantian category of *als ob* (as though, as if), the figure installs in writing the possibility of imagining a relation between experience or fact and a fictionalised experience. Thus the figure names a certain analogical, rather than mimetic, correspondence. The *as if* names a 'fictional' condition, an imagined and therefore *phantasmatic* possibility that is not a lie, but which either has not happened or which, more significantly, cannot be experienced as such. So, I cannot experience 'my death'. I can experience dying, but what I call my death is not available to me. The death which I call 'mine' is never mine, properly speaking: it is the impossible, unavailable (like language) to appropriation. *As if* institutes a form of 'hinge' between the possible and the impossible. It names the spectral condition of imagination as the projection of fictions, the poetic and narratives: it figures and plays on, possibly, the literary itself. So I can imagine a condition of being after death and yet still having consciousness of the *post-mortem*. Such an imagined condition is possible through the *as if*. To think this impossibility is to say or picture, or narrate a state *as if* I were dead. This is surely a fiction if ever there was one. We imagine an exorbitant fiction in the thought of a reflexive consciousness of the absence of consciousness, the absence or, more precisely, non-existence of the *me*, the *ego*, which thinks this.

Analogy is a marvellous thing, having to do with resemblance and proportion. Questions of correspondence arise, and then of perceived similarity, though not one in which resemblance is the question. An analogy may spring to mind as a result of there being, in the eye of the perceiver, a correspondence – a communication without words, moving from one place to another, a translation of sorts – between two wholly dissimilar phenomena. The eye, and through that, the mind, apprehends in passing, a relation without relation. The significance by which the analogy comes to pass may be as a result of comparability not in appearance, but in mood, tone, timbre. That which is analogical is not logical, strictly speaking. Take photographs or portraits of yourself, for example. Seeing an image of yourself is strange for a number of reasons, not least because you are taken outside yourself. This is true whether we speak of a painting or a photograph. You see a presence, captured, fixed in place, at a given moment. Time appears frozen. A fiction of permanent presence is given you. You are there and not there, looking at a self, which though yourself is not you. That other you looks at nothing, it only gives the appearance of looking out, never seeing you at all, as though you were invisible. It is at once fixed in time and out of time completely. It captures you in the blink of an eye. Forever.

Seeing yourself in this manner, reduced to a representation of yourself, produced in the instantaneous presentation of the self reduced to an image sent out into the world and over which you have no control (except perhaps to destroy it) – it is *as if* you were dead. We are presented through our representations of ourselves and others with this uncanny recognition.

But what is perhaps the uncanniest aspect of this apprehension is not merely that the image is that of the dead person, as Roland Barthes has hypothesised. It is *as if* in standing outside yourself you, the 'living' you, is a ghost. It is a matter of being acted on, agitated and solicited. Confronted by the simulacrum of a presence, the power of its representation imitating life and offering you a memory of yourself as a trace of your being in that representation, you may feel as you would *as if* you could experience your death. You may experience the sensation of experiencing the impossible. It is *as if* you were living on beyond 'your' death, to find yourself having become the spectral visitant, the *revenant*, who returns to the place of living and who can no longer take part in that scene. The analogy is not in the resemblance, between 'original' and 'copy'. It is in the experience of seeing yourself as others see you. It follows that you see yourself as you will be remembered. As you are remembered by others, if you are remembered, when you are absent. Your physical absence is structurally analogous to your being dead. In memory, everything happens, everything returns, and recurs, *as if*.

THE VILLAGE

Thunder throws around the sky
Tormenting the unweighted

Airborne, the instant,
Bullets of atmosphere
Driving hard upon the pane

Furious, ridiculous:
You are
A splinter in the clot

A rattling, to agitate, to irritate:
The appalling

Everything is gathered,
Gathering again,
Small circles in a pool, carried,
Force of suction,
Into a sinkhole

The inability to speak,
The failure to save another

Blood washing away
Whiteness of Victorian enamel;
Water runs to a timepiece,
Heavy-laden tock

Breaking the bell jar
An inrush of grosser air
Purity of purpose contaminated
Enlarged, diluted

Endless quiet of a village
Intruded on by sound
Not of its time

The shape of the world resumes
The village was

                Is

                        And will stay the same
Time closes over the wound that ruptures the world

COMMUNITY

'Community' is a tale we tell ourselves we need, to give us place and strength in something tangibly near, material and real, apparently, and larger than ourselves. We equate community with the materiality of location, itself given a singular identity through the agency of the proper name. So: a village; a settlement given a personal pronoun, which binds the various parts, the streets, the houses, farms, shops.

Community is the name that announces the apparent binding of the disparate elements and the human beings who dwell there, work there, interacting with one another, as one (*comme une*). As if there were unity merely as a result of chance gatherings, heapings up, accumulation. In any village the graveyard is the most appropriate visual metaphor for a community, every individual, slightly differentiated by this marker, that headstone, but all laid together, surrounded often by a wall, or fence, some boundary that marks and demarcates inclusion and exclusion, the binding force both the plot of land, sanctioned as having its own identity according to, in this example, religion, the idea, the history, and the practice. Community is therefore both material and spiritual.

Community, the idea of its maintenance, is implicitly reliant on fair weather. There is an atmospherics, a climatic status quo necessary for the illusion of community. We tend towards the thought that with community comes the minimisation of change, of transformation. Where alteration for the common good (supposedly) takes place, it is justified, both in advance and in retrospect, by the idea that change is merely concerned with nothing changing, that difference is minimised, sameness supplemented.

Absolute climate control is impossible, though. There is often a climacteric that countersigns climate control, a critical period or event, where ripening reaches a critical turn or dehiscence, and the world of 'community' bursts open, undergoing a transformation, permanent or temporary. Such crisis leaves the signs of its eruption, interruption. Nothing is 'as one' any longer. Or rather, this: the taking place, the coming to pass of the climacteric in whatever form that may assume is just the event that reveals a difference within, contrary to the assumption of sameness, which was always already immanent in the possibility of the same. There is no community that can exclude difference. Community is only thinkable because a difference is suppressed, waiting to return.

Baltic Correspondance / Bałtycka Korespondencja

1. AN ARMFUL, YOURS / NARĘCZE, TWOJE

The motion, effortless,
Extending, gathering speed
In early light, flight achieving
Step barely grounded,
A brief backward glance,
Then the flow, the forward grace –
L'avenir, je t'embrasse.

Walter must have looked from his window
Caught halting in mid-composition,
Astounded at the sight.

You bring me words,
Armfuls of sound, and cadence;
Laughing, you pour upon my head
Light amber, glowing golden rhythms
Illuminating the dark corners,
Infusing with a breath,
As it was thought the older gods once did,
Divine afflatus, ghostly inrush.

TRANSLATION

Correspon*dance*: no, you are not misreading this; no, this is not a misspelling. The spelling is French, though homophonically bearing a similarity to its English cousin. Yet, in English, were I to insist on the use of 'a' instead of 'e', I would not only, quite possibly, be signalling Derrida's use of 'a' instead of 'e' in the spelling of 'différance', by which he chose to mark and remark that which, in writing, escapes any voicing, thereby performing the manner in which writing is irreducible to voice; I would also be insisting on a certain dance that takes place between two, two languages, or the one who corresponds, in all senses, with the other. Writing is there already, in the motion between the one and the other. Writing does not come after voice, as philosophy insists. The privilege given to voice, and therefore to presence in philosophy – as though the philosophers had never written – is called by Derrida phonocentrism, and logocentrism also.

Swobodny ruch
Przyspiesza, nabiera rozpędu
We wczesnym świetle, osiągający lot
Krok tylko lekko przyciągany,
Krótkie spojrzenie wstecz,
Potem płynny pęd, dalsza łaska –
L'avenir, je t'embrasse.

Walter zapewne wyjrzał przez okno,
przystanął niepewnie w środku zdania,
Zdumiony widokiem.

Przynosisz mi słowa,
Naręcza dźwięków i kadencji;
Śmiejąc się, polewasz moją głowę
Jasnym bursztynem, rozżarzonymi złotymi rytmami,
Które rozświetlają ciemne kąty,
Tchnąc oddech,
Jak czynili to bogowie dawniej,
Boska weno, widmowe wtargnięcie.

The privilege, from Plato on, given to voice, and with that, the philosophical distrust of, and occasionally ambivalence in the face of, writing, is a convenient fiction. (The distrust of writing arises because writing does not rely on the presence of the author. Writing can be interpreted in the author's absence, and therefore may be misinterpreted, translated in a manner that goes against the conscious intent of the writer; meaning may go astray, writing being capable of acts of betrayal, or dehiscence, spilling a seed in excess of generation).

So, the privilege given to voice is a tale; the story of voice the philosopher tells to himself. The tale says there is no need of writing, for the words spoken by the philosopher should bear their meaning self-evidently, with an immediacy not open to interpretive slippage. There should be a match so exact between the spoken word and the thing signified that correspondence is absolute, as if – imagine the fiction – there were no separation, no division at all, between signifier and signified.

[continues

2. BALTIC / BAŁTYK

I thought of the Baltic one summer's day
Sitting in gridlock in Southern California.
The overheated days coalesced –
Asphalt softening, pooling in radiant light,
A blackness holding viscous on the shoe.
(Had you been poor enough to walk)

I remembered the lamp she held
Stepping, barefoot, through the firs,
Her sinister hand clutching at a bear
That would no longer growl.

Too hot for sleep,
Too dark for day, too light for night,
The longer summer of another age,
A nightgown already intimate with sweat.

Memory sought to tear itself,
Being grasped so rudely by an unsuspecting present
Intent on penetration, careless
Of a Northern breeze.

The other motorists failed to understand
Why the car in which I sat
Found itself
Incapable of onward motion,
Remaining stalled in the thought
Of the Baltic shore.

Writing marks speech however with an ineffaceable if silent trace, a trait, a mark of translation and betrayal simultaneously, in even the most faithful translation. There is always already a supplement, that is to say, both a replacement and an addition.

This is writing's secret, a secret everywhere, speaking in a silent tongue, which the philosopher cannot make mute, because writing is already without voice, until received by some recipient, someone who arrives to read, and so speak in this, the voice of the other, a voice that is not a voice at all.

So, correspon*dance*, as if, in that *a*, in the remark of différance, there is silent acknowledgement, a response that says yes to the deconstruction of phonocentric privilege.

And, at (not quite) the same time, all such matters being a question of the temporal and spatial differentiation by which writing comes into play, there is also the more playful acknowledgement of all those things that the French signals: concordance, or match, relationship between, the exchange of letters, the entering into or being in correspondence with another.

Pewnego letniego dnia myślałem o Bałtyku,
Stojąc w korku w południowej Kaliforni.
Przegrzane dni zlewały się w jedno –
Asfalt miękł, stapiał się w promiennym świetle,
Czerń kleiła się do buta.
(Jeśli nie stać cię było na samochód)

Przypomniałem sobie, jak trzymała lampę
Krocząc boso pośród jodeł,
Lęworęcznie uczepiona niedźwiedzia,
Który już nie ryczał.

Za gorąco na sen.
Za ciemno na dzień, za jasno na noc,
Dłuższe lato innych czasów,
Koszula nocna bliska już od potu.

Wspomnienie szarpało się,
Tak nagle schwycone przez teraźniejszość, która
Niczego nie podejrzewając zdecydowała się wtargnąć,
Nie zważając na północą bryzę.

Inni kierowcy nie rozumieli
Dlaczego samochód, w którym byłem
Okazał się
Niezdolny, by ruszyć do przodu,
Zgaszony myślą
O brzegu Bałtyku.

[continues

3. YOU SEND ME PHOTOGRAPHS / PRZYSYŁASZ MI ZDJĘCIA

You send me photographs
Of a cold and northern sea
I once knew
Before you were born,
Because I had to suffer
Economics.

The light, steel to grey.
Beautiful whites, silver
Sharpening in clearer blues,
Too many words for which
I sought to spill
Across my tongue
Hurriedly,
A wave smashed,
Beach breaking
Roil, surf, turn, pitch.
Shiver.

Beryl, cobalt, indigo
And teal I give you back
So gratefully. They
Roll from my tongue
Smooth polished
Over the coming tide.

In short, the *dance* of communication, of what corresponds and what remains behind in any translation; in (let me insist on this, allow me to pursue the strong reading, betraying as I do my own 'tongue', what I call 'my own tongue', through the playful accommodation of the other's tongue in my mouth, which here, in writing slips by, positioning itself more or less silently) a correspondence between the one and the other (the poet and translator, the lover and the beloved, say), the one being undone in its supposed unicity by the act of corresponding, the one become the other of the other.

Przysyłasz mi zdjęcia
Zimnego, północnego morza,
Które kiedyś znałem
Przed twoimi narodzinami,
Bo musiałem znosić
Ekonomię.

Światło szare, stalowe,
Piękne biele, srebro
Wyostrzone w czystych błękitach,
Zbyt wiele słów, których
Szukałem rozlało się
Po moim języku
Pospiesznie,
Rozbita o brzeg fala,
Wzburzenie, piana, zwrot, szczyt.
Dreszcz.

Beryl, kobalt, indygo
I zielonomodry oddaję ci
Z wdzięcznością. One
staczają się z mojego języka
Gładkie, wypolerowane
Przez nadchodzącą falę
przypływu.

What then is translation? Or rather, let me ask, without the hope of an answer, what manner of act is translation? This is a different question entirely. I am not proposing to suggest what is a good translation, a faithful translation, a translation involving a matter of fidelity.

There is always a matter of correspondence or *correspondence* to be sure, and the reader will doubtless admire some of the work of translation, the 'art' of translation perhaps, in reading the present volume, while deploring other efforts as being wide of the mark, to use an idiom that will certainly remain untranslatable in some languages.

The mark (of translation and betrayal, signaled in that *a*) is there. This offers a figure for the trait, that which remains in any writing but beyond translation (even if one is talking of communication in a single language); but – and this I think is the essence of a certain translation – it, the trace remains, as the mark, remarking the mark of what we call the 'original' language, inasmuch as it is not the mark that the translation becomes the figure of, a palimpsest set adrift, irreconcilable with that which engendered its becoming. Irreducible to apprehension, there is always that sign of an otherness, which I only barely glimpse, after which I grasp.

[continues

4. BARN OWL AND FOX GLOVE / PŁOMYKÓWKA I NAPARSTNICA

Early mornings in the rain
A scarab hurries
Away
Across the silences
Of a French poet's tongue
Between us

The seller of raspberries laughs
At my face
Burying, (embedded)
Burrowing (nestled)
Into your polka dot scarf.

(And I think of Leonard Cohen)

Here and there,
A handful of cherries
Wind tumbled;
The summer rain
Making mischief;

The scent of jasmine
Burdens the afternoon.
Swift, above, skywriting
Hedgehog hurrying
Close to the hedgerow.

Along the petiole.
See, closely,
A raindrop stalled;
A beetle runs.
Starlings fall to ground
To eat voraciously.
The scent of the vixen
Reaches my nostrils
Through half-slipping sleep,
As, I imagine,
An armful of hay,
Grasped carelessly
While a hand, hers
Descending, with a petal touch
Brushes away a forelock.

Not to awaken, this would be the dream.

Wczesne poranki w deszczu
Skarabeusz przemyka
pośpiesznie
Przez cisze
We francuskim języku poety
Między nami

Sprzedawca malin śmieje się
Z mojej twarzy
Wtopionej
Wtulonej
W twój szal w groszki.

(A ja myślę o Leonardzie Cohenie)

But then, not every reader will be able to read every translation, and not equally so. The signs of translation are everywhere, as resistant as they are sympathetic, even when, especially when, one knows, or thinks one knows, the language in question.

The translator, says Derrida, has a "beautiful and terrifying responsibility", an "insolvent duty and debt without ceasing to tell himself [or herself, it ought to be remarked, especially in the present case] 'never ever again'".

I want to shy away from commitment and comment; I desire this in the face of the anxiety caused by what I feel to be the impossibility of doing justice to an adequate reading. Let me retreat behind authority therefore, while treating of translation, in the 'voice' of another, once more, Derrida, for whom translation:

"…was always, in me, the other face of a jealous and admiring love, a passion for what summons, loves, provokes and defies translation while running up an infinite debt in its service, an admiration for those…who, to my mind, are the only ones who know how to read and write – translators. Which is another way of recognizing a summons to translation at the very threshold of all reading-writing. Hence the infinity of loss, the insolvent debt."

Gdzieniegdzie
Garście czereśni, co
Strącił wiatr;
Letni deszcz
Psoci;

Zapach jaśminu
Obarcza popołudnie.
Powyżej jerzyk kreśli znaki
Na niebie, jeż mknie.

Wzdłuż żywopłotu.
Spójrz: szypułka,
Wokół niej
Kropla zastygła;
Żuk przebiegł.
Szpaki spadają na ziemię
By jeść łapczywie.
Woń lisicy
Sięga moich nozdrzy
Przez półsen, gdy
Wyobrażam sobie
Naręcze siana,
Schwycone niedbale,
A dłoń
jej
Opada – płatek dotyku –
I odgarnia kosmyk.

Nie przebudzić się, to byłby sen.

All translation (even that which we call reading, for this too is a translation, as I have already insisted) only has its chance that its correspondence will be received, that it will have arrived, and that there will be some correspondence between the one and the other, the written and the read; the "idiomatic singularity… where a passion for translation comes to lick it as a flame or amorous tongue might" have been apprehended, realised, in translation (though this remains only a chance), that motion where reading becomes a writing to be read, wherein the tongue of the other comes as close as possible, "while refusing at the last moment to threaten or to reduce, to consume or to consummate, leaving the other body intact but not without causing the other to appear". (Derrida, 'What is a Relevant Translation' 2001, 174-200)

[continues

5. SEHNSUCHT / SEHNSUCHT

"Nothing is comparable,
Nothing so serious has been or will be again."
– David Constantine

I was aware, at first, of wood,
Long panels lining walls –
And booths, small, sheltered,
Dark, discrete; and you.
Or should I say, your eyes?
The memory suggests
A gaze, unwavering, welcoming
Warm, deep, liquid, daring me
To confession or to spill a secret;
Just for you, you made it seem,
I think, in retrospect.

How we had come here was unknown,
At this table, in the corner, shaded
Out of view, to 'tryst'
Old-fashioned word, self-consciously half laughed,
A meeting pre-arranged
In the unconscious – yours or mine? –
For strudel and vanilla sauce;
A European café
Kafka would approve the ambiguities,
Benjamin the architecture, the design;
Burnside would unravel
The histories in the dawning of the moment,
An event, suspended in the telling,
Captured vis-à-vis
All that, passing strangely, in-between
Remained indefinite as to time
But all too briefly there and gone,
Come to pass.

C'est entre nous:
Between the eye and the blink,
Between the whisper and the silence
Between the first unheard,
Then, softly though insistently, repetition en plein air
Somehow, years later, hours or an instant
– How long? Who can tell?
– I had stepped away.
Looking back, I saw you there, sitting patiently,

[continues

„Nic nie jest porównywalne,
Nic równie poważnego nie wydarzyło się ani znów się nie wydarzy."
– David Constantine

Najpierw dostrzegłem drewno,
Długie deski na ścianach –
I stoliki, małe, osłonięte,
Ciemne, dyskretne; i ty,
A może powinienem powiedzieć: twoje oczy?
Pamięć podpowiada
Spojrzenie uporczywe, serdeczne,
Ciepłe, głębokie, płynne, ośmielające
Spowiedź lub wyznanie tajemnicy;
Tylko tobie,
Myślę z perspektywy czasu.

Jak znaleźliśmy się tu nie wiadomo,
Przy tym stoliku w rogu, osłonięci
Poza wzrokiem: „schadzka"
Staroświeckie słowo, pokryte nieśmiało śmiechem,
Spotkanie umówione
W podświadomości – twojej czy mojej? –
Na strudel z sosem waniliowym;
Europejska kawiarnia
Kafka pochwaliłby wieloznaczności,
Benjamin architekturę, projekt,
Burnside rozwinąłby
Historie u zarania tej chwili,
Wydarzenie, zawieszone w opowieści,
Uchwycone wobec
Tego wszystkiego, zachodzące dziwnie, pomiędzy
Pozostało nieokreślone w czasie,
Obecne zbyt krótko, by zaraz zniknąć,
Przeminąć.

C'est entre nous:
Pomiędzy okiem a mgnieniem,
Pomiędzy szeptem a ciszą,
Pomiędzy pierwszym nieusłyszanym,
Potem cichym, lecz uporczywym powtórzeniem en plein air
Lata, godziny czy chwilę później
– Jak długo? Kto to wie?
– Odszedłem.
Gdy spojrzałem za siebie, zobaczyłem cię tam: siedziałaś cierpliwie,

One language, says Derrida of the act of translation, licks another, as if it were a caress, as if correspondence were this amorous dance.

What is not a translation? Nothing!

What is a translation? Everything!

[continues

Head turned away and down.
Regret and longing in equal measure
Stole upon me
As I stepped into the elevator,
As you became she,
A moment's slip from tense to tense,
Just another figure in a story to be told
A memory to persist, to call, to nag unceasingly
At the edges of my sleep.
(At the table, in the corner, she sits waiting,
All alone in Oslo,
A Berlin winter's morning,
Unter den Linden,
"In der Mitte der Mitte",
She might have laughed at the obvious pun
– Or all alone in Budapest on Christmas Eve...)
All the stories became one in that instant, and so lost,
The trace for which there remains only, what's the word?

Z głową odwróconą, pochyloną.
Żal i tęsknota w równej mierze
Podkradły się do mnie,
Gdy wsiadałem do windy,
Gdy zmieniłaś się w nią,
Uskok chwili z czasu w czas,
Kolejna postać z opowieści do opowiedzenia
Wspomnienie, które nie ustępuje, woła, dręczy nieustannie
Na obrzeżach mojego snu.
(Przy stoliku w rogu ona siedzi i czeka,
Całkiem sama w Oslo,
Zimowy poranek w Berlinie
Unter den Linden,
„In der Mitte der Mitte",
Może zaśmiałaby się z oczywistej gry słów
– Lub całkiem sama w Wigilię w Budapeszcie...)
W tamtej chwili wszystkie opowieści stały się jedną i tak utracony
Ślad pozostaje jedynie z tego, co...no właśnie co?

This play of tongues, the dance, the touch, is admitted in any correspondence, as soon as there are correspondents, but in this dance called translation particularly. As Derrida would have us understand, the impossibility of language, its idiomatic singularity, renders all translation (both in the narrow and the expanded senses on which I have been playing) as that which is haunted in advance of the act with an infinity of loss, while at the same time, heaping unreasonably, exorbitantly, on the translator a debt it is impossible to clear.

The translator remains insolvent, guilty, as if he or she were translated in her caress, becoming in that reading-become-writing a figure from a Kafka parable. Always before the law, the translator, without having done anything, finds herself condemned, both by this love, this desire, and also the unreasonable debt. Translation is a question of crossing a sea, remaining all at sea, moving from shore to shore.

Even at the very start – starts, origins, beginnings: these too are fictions, convenient more or less by which we believe we orient ourselves in setting out for a heading the location of which we have no clear sense – the problem is stated, written down. Correspondance / Korespondencja. Already in that pun / torque, French and English trading places, corresponding approximately, but not exactly and so admitting, opening, to loss in the motion of writing, the passion and debt of translation, the reading-writing, is at work. This is compounded further by the Polish translation, which translates both French and English, but which cannot carry over, account for, or recount, the differential play.

The various possibilities, the play within any one word, the correspondences to which I have already alluded, are found across this range of Polish words:

> Korespondencja: mainly an exchange of mail
> Zgodność: agreement, compliance, also accordance
> Odpowiedniość: pertinence, appropriateness
> Stanowisko: a position or a stance

Notice how, the first aside, each of these terms has a certain 'pertinence', an 'appropriateness', each takes a position or stance regarding the idea of translation.

[continues

6. READ / CZYTAJ

Read the poem as if you had never seen it before
Rediscover the words as if this were a hand never seen before
There is something in you that wants to be moved
This very desire waits in your solitude
While most invent solutions that are easy
While you and I know to trust what is difficult
The difficult is the most alive
Spontaneous and in all opposition
Knowing little we must trust in what is difficult
This will never abandon us
The difficult is the reason for us to trust
It is also good to love
Because love is difficult
The poet says this
For one human being to love another human being
This is perhaps the most difficult task
The final test and proof
For which all other work is merely preparation
Young people are incapable of love
It is something they must learn
Learning is long solitary anxious
And moves with an open vulnerable heart
Surrendering to a solitude heightened and profound
Loving is not to merge not to unite
But to become open
To become something other
To become world in himself for the other
Some other calling and appealing
From great distances however close
Demanding
For love human lives are barely enough
What can life do with a heap of broken images
Mistaken for communion?
So each of us loses himself for the sake of the other
Losing the other and each and every other who remained
To come
To love is to maintain one's solitude
To live in the depths of a buried aloneness
Endure and take on every day the difficult work of love
As a burden
As an apprenticeship
As a travail
Do not succumb to the frivolous game

Translation is always, when good, about accordance, compliance, agreement. This is equally true of the English word, and the French. Each word, in every language, corresponds to, and with, the other, even as each, in its correspondence, in the manner of its speaking of and to every other, is tattooed by what it is not, by that infinity of loss. Each word, like a tongue, comes close to, without reducing, every other, although in this approach, the intimate proximity, there is a point beyond which it can come no further. That impossibility of traversal bespeaks in silence – in the silence that every word falls into as it speaks its own sense, signing itself – the failure, the insolvency, the unpayable debt, the implicit recognition of an idiomatic singularity.

Each of these four words thus translates, or at least opens the possibility for, all language, performing the most appropriate, and it has to be said painfully poignant, sense of correspondence and translation – the sense that is nothing other than writing, the very motif and motivation of différance - that is the pulse of all language in the sense defined by Stéphane Mallarmé: "The imperfection of languages consists in their plurality; the supreme language is lacking: thinking is writing without accessories or even whispering, the immortal word remains silent; the diversity of idioms on earth prevents anyone from uttering the words which otherwise, at a single stroke, would materialise as truth."

Czytaj wiersz, jakbyś go nigdy wcześniej nie widział
Odkrywaj na nowo słowa, jakby to było pismo wcześniej niewidziane
Jest w tobie coś, co pragnie poruszenia
To właśnie pragnienie czeka w twojej samotności
Gdy inni wymyślają łatwe rozwiązania
Gdy ty i ja umiemy zaufać temu, co trudne
To, co trudne najpełniej jest żywe
Spontanicznie i wbrew wszystkiemu
Wiedząc mało musimy zaufać temu, co trudne
To nas nigdy nie opuści
To, co trudne jest dla nas powodem, by zaufać
Dobrze jest też kochać
Bo miłość jest trudna
Tak mówi poeta
Dla jednego człowieka miłość do drugiego człowieka
Jest być może najtrudniejszym zadaniem
Ostatecznym testem i dowodem
Do których cała pozostała praca to tylko przygotowanie
Młodzi ludzie niezdolni są do miłości
To coś, czego muszą się nauczyć
Nauka jest długa samotna pełna niepokoju
Odbywa się z bezbronnym otwartym sercem
Poddaje się samotności spotęgowanej, głębokiej
Kochać to nie łączyć się czy jednoczyć
Lecz stawać się otwartym
Stawać się czymś innym
Stawać się światem w sobie dla innego
Jakiegoś innego, który woła i przyciąga
Z oddali choć blisko
Domaga się
Dla miłości ludzkie życia ledwo wystarczą
Co zrobi życie ze stosem rozbitych obrazów
Pomylonych z komunią?
I tak każdy z nas traci siebie dla innego
Traci innego i każdego kolejnego innego, który miał Przyjść
Kochać to zachować swoją samotność
Żyć w bezmiarze skrytego osamotnienia
Przetrwać i każdego dnia podejmować trudny wysiłek miłości
Jak brzemię
Jak staż
Jak znój
Nie ulegać błahej grze

[continues

7. YOU, REMAIN / TY, POZOSTAJESZ

Summer hummed,
It buzzed with imagined life
Close to my ear
Something not unlike a
Voice
Played on a reel to reel
At high speed.

In the boathouse
On the bare floor
In the naked house
You lay
Dreaming of a cooler season
The Baltic freezing at the landline
Where water breaks
And silts the shore.

– Always
I am hiding out here in my dreams,
I cannot be found
The Swedish woods are far too deep; sound
It will not carry.
We could remain
We could disappear
We could lie, we could die
In one another's arms.

The heat, so close I feel
Another's skin,
Recalls your island dreams. Today

And then

A universe away, along the coastal line.

Reading then, we may wish to propose, is a mode of translation. For, if we follow Mallarmé, the imperfection of languages, the plurality they embody, and the lack, the incipient loss they confess in silence, and which arrives to haunt as soon as there is a reader for a text, reveals itself in the act of reading.

The meanings of the verb 'to read' are numerous, its origins, appropriately, obscure, as the *Oxford English Dictionary* informs us. Earliest Teutonic and Sanskrit precursors suggest acts of deliberation, consideration, giving thought or attendance to; or otherwise to succeed or to accomplish. Later definitions complicate matters. Coming back to a narrower, conventional sense of correspondence: To read 'read' necessarily dictates the necessity of openness, of being open to receiving, of being the recipient of a particular correspondence; being open to becoming the reader the text searches for in its having been mailed, sent, posted.

While up to this point I have remarked on the gap between writing and voice, and wish also to discuss briefly a relationship that has been there implicitly all along: that between text and reader. There remain to be navigated, deciphered, numerous significations, a complex web of possible meanings, a skein of traces and inscriptions within the single, and singular word. In order to be able to begin reading what it means to read, one must open oneself to the idea that what is read is only a momentary recognition, a provisional translation on the way to another. It is perhaps a fleeting response, an affirmation of a certain pulse or rhythm, shared between the text and the reader, between the one and the other. In order to stabilise that act of reading, one must always perform reading or translation with an inescapable degree of violence, a loving rendering. Something however remains; what is read is never wholly or finally translated.

Something is left behind, missed altogether, something other is yet to be read. Loss inhabits the place of translation.

Lato szumiało,
Brzęczało wyobrażonym życiem
Tuż przy moim uchu
Coś jakby
Głos
Odtwarzało szpule taśmy
Z ogromną prędkością.

W hangarze dla łodzi
Na obnażonej podłodze
W nagim domu
Leżałaś
Marząc o chłodniejszej porze,
O Bałtyku zamarzającym na styku z lądem,
Miejscu, gdzie rozbija się fala
I zamula brzeg.

– Zawsze kryję się tutaj w snach,
Gdzie nikt mnie nie odnajdzie
Szwedzki las jest zbyt głęboki; dźwięk
Go nie przeniknie.
Pozostalibyśmy
Zniknęlibyśmy
Leżelibyśmy, umarlibyśmy
W swoich ramionach.

Upał, tak blisko czuję
Skórę innego,
Przywołuje twoje wyspowe marzenia. Dziś

I wtedy

Wszechświat stąd, wzdłuż linii brzegu.

[continues

8. ROAD / DROGA

That road, up to the light,
Which once was lined with trees;
Disease had killed them all
So down they came,
Though the road, of course, remained
Vertical into the vanishing point.

You are still there,
Though the trees are gone.
Gold on green, dressed in blue
An orange blanket by an orange car.

Your name recalls the ages of the landscape
Your hair against the field
The golden flowers of the ginsterbusch
Though you, more elegantly Latinate,
Despite your temper haunted
By the blood of your mother's mother,
Through all the generations
Skjaldmær is the word.

And mine? You thought perhaps,
A weakened and corrupted remnant
Of wulfheodenas, of the peace sued for,
The wulfrith, who granted such reprise
– Or death.

We both have our thorns
That haunt, persecute and prick.
I would trade all our dead tongues
I would harrow and undo
The English-speaking world
To find my way back to you,
To speak again in silent tongues
And sing in silent music.

There is the rare and obscure transitive use of the verb. It can mean to think, to suppose. It can mean to have an idea, to guess or otherwise extrapolate by conjecture or speculation. Equally rare is the idea that reading involves an act of assuming the correspondence as given (given by whom?), which may then, in translation, be transmitted elsewhere. Slightly more familiar is the notion of reading as prediction, of foretelling or foreseeing, discerning or distinguishing.

Reading, in this sense, involves the translation of correspondence between the past transmission, and a future possibility, a reception, an interpretation to come. The sense of inspection and interpretation is relatively common. This leads to that sense of reading, where a meaning or significance is attached to an object. Translation – reading – is that act whereby, becoming open, one becomes something other. A correspondence is taken. Having arrived, the correspondence asks, invites, demands the recipient become that 'stance' or 'position' that accords to what has been received. Yet reading can also mean to leave a mark, or otherwise impress on something, such as fabric or a page, an imprint. Thus while reading in some cases attempts to be predictive, translation as reading must be more open. The translator must be the good reader, the lover, corresponding to that which the other writes on the self.

Ta droga ku światłu,
Dawniej obsadzona drzewami;
Wszystkie zabiła choroba,
Więc zniknęły,
Choć droga oczywiście pozostała
Pionowa do punktu zbiegu.

Wciąż jesteś tu,
Choć drzew już nie ma,
Złoto na zieleni, ubrana na niebiesko
Pomarańczowy koc przy pomarańczowym samochodzie.

Twoje imię przywołuje wieki krajobrazu
Twoje włosy na tle pola
Złote kwiaty ginsterbusch
Choć ty, z łaciny elegancka,
Pomimo usposobienia nawiedzanego
Przez krew matki twojej matki
Przez wszystkie pokolenia
Słowem: skjaldmær.

A moje? Może myślałaś
Słabsza, uszkodzona pozostałość
Wulfheodenas, wyproszonego pokoju,
Wulfrith, zapewnionego ułaskawienia
– lub śmierci.

Oboje mamy własne kolce,
Które prześladują i kłują.
Przeorałbym i rozpruł
Anglojęzyczny świat,
By odnaleźć drogę do ciebie,
By znów mówić niemymi językami
I śpiewać w niemej muzyce.

Reading understood thus is perceived as the response to a sign or trace, some writing, a manifestation of the other, though never the other itself. There is always a question of temporality to be considered, as much as any spacing that correspondence, writing, translation announces.

[continues

9. A MILLER'S TALE / OPOWIEŚĆ MŁYNARZA

We have ourselves a frenzied loop
And on we go, percussive;
We hammer and tattoo our lives from day to day
Inspiring the pen, the pencil, ink or lead,
The line slow ravelling,
The circle turns
With intervals and accents
Passing notes, the minor fall;
A major fifth, diminishing
Toward the end of day,
Where once
– A good friend said, touching my silence
With all the ambiguity of
The stranger who knows me better than I know myself –
The breeze, balmy air,
Lifted the branch to tap the tattoo
On the side of the barn.
Twilight still (your words form in my mouth),
I pause, then on I go, descending into
The now, the never here, which rushes
Contra posto, headlong,
Into the rhythm of a night
Phase shifted on the air, upborne,
A song that speaks of everything
In secret, in unspoken words,
And otherwise,
An afterword
An other's tongue
The tone, the tenor
– *Stimmungsträger*
The experience of mood,
So evanescent as to linger
On the outskirts of eternity.

Here comes the hurdy gurdy man, and he's singing songs of ...?

There is never one time, but always more than one time. The form to be read is not only spatial and rhythmic, it is also temporal and polyvalent. It is at once both lacking and excessive, beyond all mere recuperable polyvalence.

An even more obscure meaning for this word 'read' is in its use, not as a verb, but as a noun, signifying the stomach of an animal: the belly of the beast. This sense, the *Oxford English Dictionary* speculates (reads?) (translates?) tentatively, as being the oldest possible of recuperable meanings, older than those other senses already considered in passing.

Can we speculate a connection between the material of the stomach and the act of translation?

Can we read 'read' and 'read', reading between them a copulative and translative correspondence? How can we 'hear' the mute difference, in looking at the inscribed sign?

Or can we read there, decipher, translate, the attempted act of communication, correspondence, agreement – a certain postal transmission – on the part of the one who reads or translates?

Is there discernible the act, the process of communication, of a reading-writing?

Przygotowaliśmy sobie szaloną pętlę
I ruszamy, w rytm perkusji;
Młoteczkami wybijając, tatuując nasze życia z dnia na dzień
Inspirując ołówek, pióro, tusz czy ołów
Linia wikła się powoli,
Koło obraca
Interwały, akcenty
Ulotne nuty, raz niżej w moll;
Raz wyżej w dur
Ku kresowi dnia,
Gdzie dawniej
– Rzekł dobry przyjaciel, dotykając mojej ciszy
Z całą wieloznacznością
Obcego, który zna mnie lepiej
Niż ja znam siebie –
Bryza, balsamiczne powietrze
Uniosła gałąź, by wystukać tatuaż
Na ścianie stodoły.
Zmierzch wciąż (twoje słowa formują się w moich ustach),
Przystaję, aby ruszyć dalej, schodząc w
Teraz, nigdy tutaj, co gna
W kontrapoście, na łeb na szyję
W rytm nocy,
Przesunięcie fazowe w powietrzu, nienarodzona
Pieśń, która mówi o wszystkim
W tajemnicy, niewypowiedzianymi słowy
I inaczej,
Posłowie,
Język innego,
Ton, brzmienie
– Stimmungsträger
Doświadczenie nastroju,
Tak ulotne, że trwa
Na obrzeżach wieczności.

Nadchodzi kataryniarz, by śpiewać piosenki o...?

[continues

10. KASHUBIA / KASZUBY

A ghost in the window
                        Hovers behind

The elderly
      Though serious, because German
Writer

As the Irish poet
            Murmurs
"a little sadly"

With this there is, there remains, discernibly there, the concomitant opening – inevitably – of a gap certainly, and perhaps also an aporia between the 'read' (of the animal) and the 'reading', between the 'reading' and what is 'read'. It is in this space, this 'between', and the loss that separates as much as it joins, that readers find themselves as possible translators, always indebted, always guilty, insolvent, and yet confessing love, desire, the intimacy of correspondence. Which still leaves us with remains to be read.

The English words 'remain' or 'remains' have specific resonances that loosen our grasp on any perceived significance, and which only become tightened with the context in which they are found, as if they were insects trapped briefly in a spider's web.

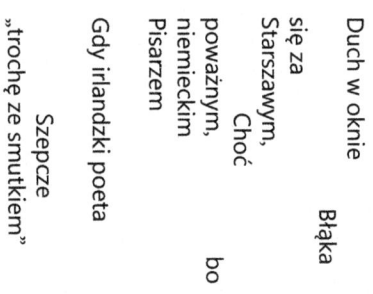

However, even though we use a word with a particular signification in mind, there remains in that word, with its intended, conscious signification, the remains of the other meanings. Those meanings remain encrypted. The idea of remains – the trace, the forensic, corporeal, or historical remainder – is not simply a reference to the past.

For something can always 'remain to come'; it 'remains to be seen', as the idiom, indicative of an uncertain future event, has it. And even as there are 'remains', artefacts, phenomena – memories too perhaps – so too, that which remains, as remains – the trace of the past constantly with us, of the past and yet in in the now, remaining now – is/are also that which we find remaining. For this perception of that which is just remaining is, as the word-cluster implies, a reminder, an aide-mémoire, a souvenir, a memo, memento mori.

You – the other – remain(s).

The remains of the other. This is a double genitive. On the one hand, the remains, the traces, these are all that is left of the other. On the other hand, the other gives us, as a gift, the remains for which she is responsible, to which she, in turn, has borne witness, and continues so to do, implicating us, folding us (the *pli-* in 'implicate' names the fold) in the act of attestation, for which we in turn become responsible, one in a continuous weave of witnessing. And so it goes.

[continues

11. OWL AND MULLEIN / SÓWKA I DZIEWANNA

Voiceless, when pronounced,
I read your body.
Dawn, rustling, wakes
Cornflower and spruce.
Bubo.
Strigidae naps
As Aegithalos begins to sing.
Tracing the woolly leaves, tall spikes of flower
Yellowsoft touching to the air,
Forest fingers drowsing
Along the hollows.
Euonymus – a good name
For what is felt unspeakingly at first light,
Hairslide among the undergrowth.
I write you, so you do not understand.

We remain within an inescapable and asymmetrical tension, at the heart of the very thing we name in speaking of one who remains. You, the title says, remain. The other that you are, remains. The remains that you are, in writing, so many traces. These are what remain. These are remains. They remain to come, to be read, to be translated, every time the book is opened, is read, book become text in the act of reading.

Bezdźwięczne w wymowie
Czytam twoje ciało.
Brzask szelestem budzi
Chabra i świerk.
Bubo.
Strigidae drzemie,
Aegithalos rozpoczyna pieśń.
Obrysowując omszałe liście, kłosy kwiatów
Miękkozłote dotykają powietrza,
Caladenia sylvicola przysypia
Wokół dziupli.
Euonymus – dobra nazwa
Na niewyrażalne doznane z pierwszym blaskiem,
Wsuwka w poszyciu.
Piszę do ciebie, byś nie zrozumiała.

And more.

For, at the same time as the title, 'You, Remain' states 'you remain' (ignore briefly the comma, the silent mark that has an eloquence more profound than any voice can articulate), so, and this is in the work of the silence, inscription itself, the play, the torque of what Derrida calls *écriture* (not just in the narrow sense of writing, marks on a page or screen, but the very process by which meaning is produced; voice is, too, a writing, because it only has its transmissibility through spacing, structure, and so forth, and these are all signs of writing, not voice) maintains the difference that effects the deconstruction of any univocal meaning. The comma is the sign, the trait by which writing deconstructs voice, articulates and disarticulates, in a silent music of inscription. Any logocentric illusion of presence is understood as haunted and undone simultaneously by past and future of the trait, its transmission, that which makes reading possible, and it's reception, reading's being aware of the silent mark. There, in that comma, or this dash, through the articulation of that silent rupture, the mark prevents and prohibits any fullness. The one and the other remain suspended around a fulcrum.

You, the other is told, in an act of conjuring, this attempt to have some power over the other, however futile; 'you' are told: you – remain. You stay with me, you return, but you, who must remain despite any conjuration, any exorcism, you must remain *there*, not here, separate, and apart, remaining, but unable to return as such. There is never a 'here' for the other. However small the mark, writing insists on a spacing, on difference which makes communication possible, but which forestalls absolute presence. Even in the most proximal intimacy of two lovers, the other can never be 'here', where 'I' is, where 'I' understands and represents itself to itself. And this is not just the effect of writing in the narrow sense. To understand this properly, writing names that which is written on the body, writing and difference being terms for the experience of Being. Or, to quote Peter Hammill: "In the here and now, between sensation at the nerve ends and the arrival of information at the cortex, time elapses. So, you see, each time we touch, we did so in the past" ('Now Lover', 1986). Joyce too recognised this irreducible 'writing' of space become time, and time become space in *Ulysses*. Aristotle saw it only as a problem, an undecidable to do with the 'now'.

[continues

12. CHAUCHAT TRIPTYCH / TRYPTYK CHAUCHAT

I. Small blue boots,
                       dance
Laughing in the rain
                                eyes flash

Shiver with delight
The thought
                      puddles rippling

With the merest scent
Of cedar
                              vetiver
Underlined with musk
A time's moment caught
In amber

II. You came,
              You returned
Bright pools child happy

(Memories of the rain
In widened orbits)
    A gift, unlooked for
In black and indigo

III. I shall call you
                        Raspberry girl
Fruits drenched in raindrops
Laughing eyes

        celadon in hue
    (a wash, a tint, a trick
      of morning light
                    thunder's refraction

and the daylight yellowed)
And you will cause my words
To fail me once more
                        as
I look into the heart of light,
In silence I know nothing

And am consumed

I.
Błękitne buciki
    tańczcie
Śmiejąc się w deszczu
      oczy błyskają
Drżą z rozkoszy
Myśl
      marszczy kałuże
Subtelnym zapachem
Cedru
     wetiwerii
Podszyty piżmem
Chwila czasu uchwycona
W bursztynie

II.
Przyszłaś
   Wróciłaś
Błyszczące sadzawki dziecięcoszczęśliwe
(Wspomnienia deszczu
W szeroko otwartych orbitach)
     Niespodziewany dar
W czerni i indigo

III. Będę cię nazywał
    Malinową dziewczyną
Owoce przesiąknięte kroplami deszczu
Roześmiane oczy
   w odcieniu seledynowym
   (zabarwienie, odcień, świetlna
     sztuczka o poranku
      refrakcja grzmotu
pożółkłeświatłodzienne)
I sprawisz, że słowa
zawiodą
mnie raz jeszcze
    gdy
Patrzę w samo serce światła,
W ciszę
Nie wiem nic

Spalam się

The desire for raspberries was too much. She craved the fruit with such intensity that even the rain, drenching the world in a hostile flood was to be challenged that early autumn day. Or, it seemed like autumn, the weather out of line with the expectation of the time. But there were gifts, scenting the air, aromas from the park on day release from the previous days' stifling summer dryness.

Her eyes, reflecting puddles gathering around the root systems of the olive trees, stretched wide in delight, in the joy of such tinted giddiness.

The image is translated from the eye, translating the pool, translating the gathering of raindrops, precipitation become the ink in which the trace persists, returns, and waters the writer's imagination, giving the chance to the thought of fruits that would leave the tongue silenced.

[continues

13. SAME SKY / TO SAMO NIEBO

St Catherine to Sopot,
Lighthouses keep the key;
It's the same sky shared
Connecting, a dome,
An overvaulting absence
Painted blue
A finer aquatint.

The wheel turning tortures
The imagination, as
Stitching the distances
Vadstena, landfall
Reversing a Viking track
Back tracing the
1000-year-old path.

To take the lower, deeper blue,
Baltic meniscus;
And so to sail, to strive,
To float among ice floe
Wind chapping, slapping the face
In rebuke.
Until the skies are joined.

Ptolemy was the first to mention the Isle of Wight, in his *Geography*, long before St Catherine's Lighthouse came to be. The Island itself had been, according to Caesar, taken by the Belgae. Called Vectis originally, the Island was subsequently a Jutish kingdom, ruled by King Stuf, until invaded by Wulfhere of Mercia, and converted to Christianity, later to become part of Wessex under Caedwalla.

St Catherine's Lighthouse was amongst the first such installations in the British Isles, a light established there by order of the Pope in 1323. Originally, a part of St Catherine's Oratory, the octagonal tower of the original lighthouse remains, though the present working lighthouse, built in 1838, is situated near the village of Niton.

Sopot (Sopòt in Kashubian, Zoppot in German) is a coastal resort in Pomerania, on the Baltic coast. Boasting the longest wooden pier in Europe, it is known as a health spa and has a bromide spring water fountain, known as the 'inhalation mushroom'. The name is supposed to have developed from old Slavic, meaning 'stream' or 'spring', and is believed, by some, to be onomatopoeic, mimicking the murmur of water flowing to the Baltic Sea. The lighthouse, built in 1903-04, part of the Balneological Institute, was designed to hide the boiler room of the institute, and not considered a 'real' lighthouse due to the limited range of its light. Following installation of a lighting system in 1977, it assumed its present day function.

Balneology is the treatment of disease by bathing in mineral waters, usually at spas, and is considered distinct from hydrotherapy.

Z St Catherine do Sopotu,
Latarnie są kluczem;
To samo wspólne niebo,
Łączące, kopuła,
Wysklepiona nieobecność
Pomalowana na niebiesko
Piękniejsza akwatinta.

Koło obraca się, torturuje
Wyobraźnię,
Zszywając dystanse
Vadstena, ląd,
Odtwarzając trasę Wikingów,
Przemierzając wstecz
Tysiącletnią drogę.

By ruszyć niższym, głębszym błękitem,
Bałtyckim meniskiem;
I tak żeglować, zmagać się,
Dryfować pośród kry
Wiatr smaga, okłada twarz
W przyganie.
Aż nieba się złączą.

[continues

14. PROPER NAMES / NAZWY WŁASNE

It becomes clear
You wear

        Invisibly

Your furlined coat

It is there, where you are
Always, and

        Inevitably

Even when you are naked

    Or is it sheepskin?

Asked the wolf

Crossing borders,
    One tongue in the mouth of another

To staje się jasne
Nosisz
                Niewidzialnie

Swój futrzany płaszcz

Jest tam, gdzie ty
Zawsze i
                Nieuchronnie
Nawet, gdy jesteś naga

        A może to owcza skóra

Zapytał wilk

Przekraczając granice,
           Jeden język w ustach innego

Such is the effect of translation that we are often unaware of the manner of its encryptions. Words for things, for acts, events, trades, crafts, occupations, all become 'translated', even within their own language, to pass from the function to the person, and to remain thus, long after that person's ancestors have abandoned the profession, lost the skill by which their surname countersigns them, as if it were the visible ghost of their forebears' way of being in the word. So Wright, or Turner, for example, in English. Language carries what we were, long before we existed, to us, imprinting us with the sign of our having been otherwise than we remain. Today the name persists on the individual, as though in some present we existed, the feeble remnant captured in the prehensile signature.

Il devient evident
Tu portes

        Invisiblement

Ton manteau double de fourrure

Il est là, là où tu es
Toujours, et

        Inévitablement

Même lorsque tu es nue

        Ou est-il peau de mouton?
A demandé le loup

Franchir les frontières,
        Une langue dans la bouche d'un autre.

THE POET, TRANSLATED

(With no Apologies to T. S. Eliot)

The scent of limes announces home is near,
The damp, the dark of day, an autumn afternoon.
The tram, metallic scraping, halts nearby,
As hurriedly, she crosses at the light; the gloom
Slowly descending on the hills, cathedral spire
Part hidden in the trees; a scratching sound
The barrel of the lock, the tumbling of the pins,
A hand, ungloved, withdraws the well-worn key.
She hurries to the stairs, hastening ascent in lighter steps
Uneven in the turns, though still that grace
That speaks anticipation, pleasure sought,
A quiet smile, which, in the shadows, passes
On her face.
                    She puts no record on the gramophone,
But, taking off her coat, so red, so bright,
And flung, a fallen poppy petal there;
The kettle is turned on, as is a softly amber light,
– 'Finnish', she would tell you, were you there –
the tea ritually prepared, one spoon, then two:
Green, or, mildly fragrant, bergamot
Suggesting other landscapes to the south,
Calabrian hills recalled, where orange groves
In winter bear such fruit as give to northern shores
A bitter citrus tang, with which to soften and suffuse
This quiet room.
                Shoes removed,
Abandoned in the hall; a shawl is fetched,
A book, perhaps bilingual, poetry: a Polish poet,
Who could have crawled, she writes, bescaled
From under another tree, but instead, affirms
A singularity: "Jestem kim jestem" runs the line:
I am who I am; this strikes a chord,
As, pausing for reflection, slicing cake,
The fork resisted, then she stops.
      The plate put down, the book placed to one side –
Still open, shaping as a chalet roof upon a favourite restaurant,
Their timbers burgundy, recalling in their shade her shawl –
She reaches swiftly for the dial, to turn; and in that moment,
A piano's notes are heard, the sea withdraws,
To surge once more upon the Baltic strand;
She settles back, her eyes half closed, she feels
The soft endearments of an absent lover's hand
Along her cheek. All the world is here, and with it
All the gathering, a moment, moments timeless in the pause
Of what is shared in silence, what held in amber light, the time
Of each encounter, each caress, with every whispered syllable,
In every act of giving, given tenderness.

HERBSTFREUDE

Balloonflower,
Velvet blue five-pointed star;
Coral Bells,
Also alumroot,
Starry Night,
Ground hugging,
Palmately lobed and purple leaved;
Daylilies
Tawny,
Orange cinnamon,
Golden needles, and
Hush Little Baby,
Peach red to golden at the heart,
Folded frill petal sensuous,
Soft skin to the touch,
Darker red veins in translucent skinfolds
Unfolding, folding back,
Intimately revealing, a floral piccadil
Phlox, pale blue and violet, erect and fragrant,
Dehiscent fruits separating explosively,
Then early blooming Autumn Joy,
Herbstfreude,
Pink to red,
Deeper dusty reds,
Succulent, dark green below;
And above all a top note of lavender.

A BEAUTIFUL DAY

Hush Little Baby belongs to the daylily or Hemerocallis genus. Its flowers, typical of the other species belonging to the genus, last no more than 24 hours, hence the Latin meaning 'lily that flowers for a day', itself derivation from the Greek, ἡμέρα (hēmera) 'day' and καλός (kalos) 'beautiful'. The flowers are used fresh or dried in Chinese cooking, and are known as golden needles. The name is lost in translation becoming the more generic *hémérocalles* in French.

Le platycodon,
Etoile velours bleu à cinq branches;
Les heuchères, palais en violet,
Et le désespoir du peintre,
La pensée à cornes
Qui étreindent le terrain, palmée lobate aux feuilles violettes,
Les hémérocalles
Fauves,
Cannelle orange,
Aiguilles d'or, et
Dors mon petit,
Rouge de pêche doré au coeur,
Falbala plié pétale voluptueux,
Peau douce au toucher,
Sombres veines rouges dans plis cutanés translucides
Floraison et refermeture,
Le phlox, bleu pâle et violet, debout et parfumé,
Les fruits déhiscents, séparation explosive,
Ensuite la floraison hâtive des orpins,
Herbstfreude,
Rose à rouge,
Rouges plus sombres et poudreuses,
Succulents, verts foncés ci-dessous;
Et au dessus de tout, une note de tête de lavande.

All of which is to say, no amount of information can tell us anything about the flower as flower. There is that which remains untranslatable, available to our senses, to our perception, and which is irreducible to terminology, to knowledge, to information. Learning is an irrelevance in the face of the untranslatable. Flowers arrive as this gift, to unveil the redundancy of knowledge; save, perhaps, and this is the merest, most tentative speculation, that we might, indirectly, analogically as it were and through the work of apophasis by which the mind has truth unveiled to it, realise all thought and knowledge as the singular expression of so many instances that come briefly into flower.

La rose est sans pourquoi.

POPPY

Corydalis, celandine,
And bloodroot;
All these your family;
Folds softly furred,
Tongue languid
Lip suffusing,
Ruby red, milky sap,
Rushing, rounded,
Petalum outspreading,
Narcotic joys,
The dream of Mneme;
Blood swept tide
Shore battered, bereft,
Embracing the promise
Of a sweeter opiate sleep.

MEMORY

Memory is, or can be, fundamentally narcissistic. We remember the other, but in doing so, we also place ourselves in relation to the other, having always already internalised that other. Whatever we do, however we recall the other, however we reach out, with thoughts, feelings and emotions; whatever the constellated arrangement, fragmentary or coherent, continuous or discontinuous, comprised of the trace, the *trait*, and every other fleeting or abiding figure that we call collectively 'memory' (and *collectively* because memory is never single, there is always more than one trope, one trace, one effect or affect to that which 'memory' acts as proper name), the image to which we hold remains within us, as Jacques Derrida argues of the work of mourning, this being its essentially narcissistic nature.

Without even bringing death into the picture – though that is unavoidable, for many reasons – all memory belongs to, and serves to constitute, a structure of enclosed 'self-other' motivated by, and haunted by the motif, of a narcissism, of more than one narcissism. This is neither good nor bad, but thinking makes it so. Memory must therefore be thought, and the difference of memory thought: "beyond internalising memory", says Derrida, "it is necessary *to think*, which is another way of remembering".

Weeping for the other, longing for the other, we place ourselves unreasonably at the centre of a universe of self, which cannibalises the other. Failing to think differently, to think the difference in memory, memory's other, we remain bounded in a nutshell, as it were. In this, we remain drugged, in a sleep of addiction to the self that would maintain our dependency. We linger in the regions of the sleep we misrecognise as our waking lives, wherein every facet of memory is a mirror in which we see ourselves refracted endlessly as the supposed loss we mistakenly apprehend as the other.

JOSEFKA

Josef K, to the ear a feminine diminutive,
His own *babcia*, *baba*, *babka*, perhaps.
Waits patiently in the cobbled street,
Ignoring the dragon that smiles like a cat.

As, next door, the glow from the radio
warms the already ochreous hue, suffused
With amber tints. The gramophone
Doesn't play, the telephone won't ring.

But this is good: a room in which
Technology, as the art of mechanical reproduction,
Announces its anachrony,
Charming the quiet space.

Encouraged to linger, to stay, to idle
Awhile in paused contemplation –
Another coffee perhaps, or cake:
Kawa i ciasto. Ciasto i kawa.

Chiasmus of the hands entwined,
In this café of lovers on a winter's day
The tryst, the appointed place,
As, silencing, the snow falls muting all the world.

SLEEP, THE SEA

Sleep, the sea, teal body
Taking whole
The self her eyes unveiled,
Consuming emptiness and loss,
Covering over griefs unwieldy,
Though showing themselves
Infrequently.

Sleep, the ocean body,
Drowning with the welcome of
A souvenir forgetfulness,
Taking up, pulling down,
To hide within a memory's wrack,
The unrequited life.

Sleep, the water's humour,
Pauses the body buoyant
Stays at its moon surface briefly
The illusions of the reflecting mind.

Gone before the realisation,
Unstitched, unhinged, undone,
Inflooding, debording, caught
For just that instance
In solution
In dissolution.

Adieu au langage
Il y va un débordement
De signification

TEAL? TEAL! (To be filed under 'if it walks like a duck...')

— So, what is it with teal?
— I'm not sure what you mean.
— It's everywhere?
— Really?
— The colour...
— So you assume.
— You're referring to the bird?
— That's for you to decide.
— But then it would make little sense in some contexts.
— Is that so very important?
— Every occasion then, a small freshwater duck, *Anas crecca* by designation.
— If you insist, a small dabbling water bird, with a chestnut coloured head and broad green eye-patches.
— That's the one, it migrates south in winter.
— And who wouldn't?
— You, for one.
— It's known to be highly gregarious...
— That's not you, then.
— With a grey nuptial plumage.
— Definitely not you.
— Let me tell you about some words and phrases, 'remiges' for example, or 'speculum feathers'. The first is from the Latin for 'oarsman', and are located on the posterior side of a wing. Imagine a bird rowing, if you can. Speculum feathers, on the other hand, often brightly coloured, in a patch, to be seen on the inner remiges of some birds.
— The common teal?
— Yes, now you come to mention it, you'll find an iridescent green area, and also, helpfully named, the green-winged teal. This though is North American, not Eurasian. The ornithologists have some argument on-going about conspecificity or somesuch.
— Well, let them, the bird wouldn't know.
— Absolutely not.
— But, it can't always be the bird?
— You think not? The consequences of misunderstanding might prove creatively fruitful.
— Poetry, like love, risks everything on swans?*
— Exactly. Teal.
— So...
— I know what you want to ask. Is it green or is it blue? Does it, does it really matter? To distinguish teal blue from teal, the former was first used as a designation in 1927. Imagine, a specifically modernist colour! And, you can equally call it 113, because that's the number of the Crayola crayon. Then teal is the colour of intercession too, for the Intercessors of the Lamb, the shade used for a scapular symbolising the community's role as intercessors between heaven, which is blue, and earth, which is green.
— Let's say goodbye to language, there's an overflow of signification, too much...
— ...and not enough.

*La poèsie, comme l'amour, risque tout sur des signes.

THE ART OF TRANSLATION

The gap should remain,
Ravelling the exquisite moment
Some things do not travel
But reside, either side the
Separated lips.

Two part, and two respond:
opening, closing, apart and together,
Whispering the filament
The ineluctable thread

From heart to heart,
Weaving, gathering, the one in the other,
Spaces left in the textile.

The gap should remain,
One tongue in the mouth of another.

LEQUEL? LAQUELLE?

L'ouverture devrait rester
Défaisante le moment exquis
Des choses ne voyagent pas
Mais résident, de chaque côté
Les lèvres détachées.

Deux se séparent, et deux répondent:
ouvrantes, fermantes, à l'écart et ensembles,
Chuchotantes le filament
le fil inéluctable

De coeur à coeur
Tissantes, glanantes, l'une en l'autre,
Les espaces laissés dans le textile.

L'ouverture devrait rester,
Une langue dans la bouche d'un autre.

THE FUR TRADER AND THE POET

Duck slide: the ice where, captured underneath,
Browned leaves assume suspension in the glass
Of morning's grip;
There bubbles form,
To dapple all the pond,
The park, a quiet world of sleeping trees
Olive branches intertwined, the path
A canopy for lovers' quiet steps,
To gardens shaped all quiet, out of time,
And sleeping houses, elegant and still.
We hold our tongues, the raven bobs its mirth
To see our winter love in frosted breath
Made visible, as if we would inscribe
Emotion in the air, around the Olive Park.

Mirabelka at the Beach

1. A CALENDAR OF CONVERGENCES

The calendars agree
The ninth month shared,
The Orthodox year begins,
Though, in the Southern Hemisphere,
It should be March,
Your birthday therefore;
– a celebration twice, north and south.

Ending as it starts
The same day twice,
No other month save May;
Every year the first day of the week
Shared with the first day of December
– my natal day –
Separated in multiples of seven,
Its dead language name,
its ghost tongue.

If 7 were 9, not six
We could agree, we would, we should.
But the time is known, fixed,
And so I wait, down counting,
Backwards moving, hurrying,
Chivvying, chasing time
Toward the instant of
Five minutes after.

If the sun refused to shine
I don't mind.

IMAGINE (or, the Truth otherwise told)

Mirabelka at the beach

Mirabelka: the Polish 'translation' of *Mirabelle*, a plum, a drupaceous fruit, identified by its small, oval shape, smooth flesh and sweet, full taste. It is used mostly for pies and jams. A small percentage is used to make *eau de vie*, a colourless fruit brandy.

Beach: Sopot, a Polish health spa and resort on the Baltic coast, boasts Europe's longest wooden pier. It is situated on the Bay of Gdańsk, between Gdańsk and Gdynia.

Orthodox year: Eastern Orthodox churches have adopted a revised Julian calendar in order to align significant dates sanctioned by that church and those of the Gregorian calendar, the ecclesiastical year beginning in September. The revised calendar was developed and proposed in 1923 by Milutin Milanković, a Serbian mathematician, and brought to an end a divergence between the Julian and Gregorian calendars that had lasted over 300 years.

Seven: the number has long been significant in most major polytheistic and monotheistic religions. Its theosophic significance is the subject of much debate. In Latin, seven is 'septem', from which comes the name of September, being originally the seventh month of the Roman year. In the astrological calendar, September is the sixth month, forming also the first part of the seventh. September marks the start of ecclesiastical year in the Eastern Orthodox Church.

Chivvy: believed to have originated 'Chevy Chase', a ballad celebrating a battle on the Scottish border in 1388, and possibly a term for a hunting cry or pursuit.

If 7 were 9, not six: a reference to 'If 6 Was 9', by Jimi Hendrix, from *Axis: Bold as Love*. The final couplet is a quotation from that song and "if the sun refused to shine", is from 'Thank You' by Led Zeppelin. Whether the line in the latter song refers to the former is unknown.

Imagine, someone comes to you and says, as if they were for the first time inventing a fiction; that is to say *finding it* as if for a first time, as if there had never been such an act before. Imagine, this person, not a complete stranger, says to you; imagine that there is a text, comprising several poems, of which you already have some acquaintance, you have read them there, across the way, on the pages opposite; and imagine, this voice continues – and it is a voice now, just a voice, your having closed your eyes in the encouragement to imagine, as if imagination, as if the fiction that imagination makes, were a dream of sorts, or the return of a memory, albeit one that you had never known, one to which you could not lay claim as your own, as belonging to you (if, indeed, memories were belongings, possessions) – imagine the text had been rewritten, and altogether otherwise. What would it read like, how would it be (you imagine) transformed, transfigured, translated? Where would the imagination begin? Where might you start to invent, imagine a fiction from the five poems that gather themselves with a single title, 'Mirabelka at the beach'? Perhaps footnotes would help, some annotation to guide you, if you like the certainty, the surety, the promise of facts, details, data, as if, here's another fiction, you were plotting a course on a map, orienting yourself to the as yet, not wholly familiar co-ordinates. I won't tell you a story then, it is not for the poet to rewrite for the reader. Poems arrive as representations, equivocal, encrypted, reserving as much as they reveal, holding back as much as they allow to step forward. The poem arrives as if it were a postcard rather than a letter, everything written at the surface, and yet, so much more appearing to be said, a form of telegraph that signals in a semaphore of signs and imagines for the reader to reimagine, and so to find, what he or she might come to believe is there all along.

[continues

2. THE OLIVE PARK

Tending the plot,
Flowers, the family of temperate fruits
Tasted oftentimes on finger tips,
Though here with hawthorn, rowan, potentilla,
The gardener, mostly motionless,
Hints at an other me,
Another life, a path
In another park
I never trod, have yet to tread,
Am treading now,
Same footfalls, different steps.

A hover, a shimmer,
Concentrated stains of light,
Transpicuous in flight,
Shot through, glittering
In the air, around, above, adjacent
Where water lilies grow;
Insects, their shining lives
Evanescent in their brightest show.

Morning light, bearing
Invisibly the revelation of
Epochal calm, crepuscular and humid,
Suggestively framed in
Coronal defraction,
Beech leaves,
– *bēce* in old English, I recall,
Or *phagos*, dead tongue pebble
Washing up on this momentary shore;
edible oak –

Eye caught, sight captured,
Running to a halt,
I pause within the matutinal silence
Outforming itself
From within oppressive traffic's noise
To see, slyly, shyly arrived,
Pendant on the air, alighting grey and white,
Ardea cinerea, the Old World wader,
Named long ago in northern European tongues.

The Olive Park

The Olive Park: Oliwa is a quarter of Gdańsk, known for its park, its cathedral, and Opatów palace, a roccoco design originally the abbots' palace and now part of the Polish National Museum of Gdańsk, housing the Department of Modern Art. Oliwa became part of Prussia, as a result of the first Partition of Poland. (One recalls this from A-Level History. All that talk of Enlightened Despots.) There is so much more history, and little space here to tell. In *Die Blechtrommel*, Günter Grass writes of the route through the park that Oskar, with his parents (the mother Kashubian, the father, Mazerath, German), and Jan, the Polish post-office worker, who is really Oskar's father, take. Here is another annotation requiring further annotation. One word leads to another, the abyss opens, rather than closes. The neatly tended park fails in the face of a wilderness, uncontrollable.

Transpicuous: easily understood, lucid, transparent. From the Latin *transpicere*: 'look through'.

Ardea cinerea: the grey heron, a predatory wading bird, which can measure up to a metre tall. In Egyptian mythology, Bennu, connected to the sun, to creation, and birth, was signified as a heron, and was known as 'He who came into being by himself'; Roman mythology took the bird as a creature of divination. The vernacular word 'heron' is of unknown origin; having various old and middle English spellings, including *heronshaw*, which later became corrupted to *handsaw*, as in the line from *Hamlet*, 'I know a hawk from a handsaw' (II.ii.273). A not unrelated dialect pronunciation (and substitution for 'heron') persisting today in Norfolk is 'harnser'.

The question of the note, the reference, the annotation, is a fraught one. What requires annotation, what not? Should plants (rowan, hawthorn, potentilla) be noted; if so, to what extent? How much information is the right amount, and which kind of information is wanted? That which is obscure to one reader is transparent to another. This does not mean that one is a better reader than the other, of course. Knowledge is, obviously, various, and reading is not simply, if ever, a matter of hunting down references, understanding through locating meaning or significance. Which returns us to the question of bodies of knowledge, epistemologies, taxonomies. How much does a reader require, distinct, let us suppose – follow this particular fiction – from every other reader. Someone, not you, comes to me and says, imagine a fiction. Well, I will. I imagine a fiction, impossible perhaps, fascinating definitely (at least to me), of a book in which for every page, there is a blank page, perhaps two, three even (how many would be required? We stumble at the first hurdle). Well, imagining this, without specifying the number of blank pages, I imagine a fiction where every book, every novel or collection of poetry came with such blank pages on which the reader, every reader, that is to say every reader interested enough, with time enough and curiosity, could annotate as they wished, their own edition. Many readers do this already, writing in the margins (in pen? in pencil?) or use highlighter pen (unimaginable except as the most horrific possibility, and therefore all too easily imaginable). Perhaps post-its. And marginalia, taking the form of notes, comments, lucid, oblique, or merely brackets, to indicate a phrase, a line, a passage.

And, of course, some poems have, embedded within them, so many seeds in a pod, their own 'ecliptic' (Gr. *Ekleipein*) notes, little fertile pieces of information, scattered casually, the sense of which fails to appear (Gr. *Ekleipein*: 'fail to appear'). Take those passing references to old English, to Latin, to trees, to plants, to foliage, and also, named but unnamed in the vernacular, that bird observed in the park, one morning early.

[continues

3. A DIFFERENT BEACH

I.

Take me to a chair
On a beach, where,
I can watch grey skies
With you, and turning,
See their light reflected
In your eyes,
Only sometimes blue

II.

There were chairs
Numbered, one and two
Yours to the left.
Facing the sea,
We sat,
The space between our chairs
Too great.
The sand a desert,
The sky a heaven,
The sea foam white,
A darker teal,
And gull caw's grey,
Too vast to swim.
Salt depths sent to us each
Salt scented recollections.
Still we could not reach
Though longingly we looked for
One another, in our separate chairs.

III.

And she wondered –
Will there be a day when words do not arrive
When there is no poem
When nothing causes the heart to lose its seating?
In answer, a postcard arrived,
On which was written:
Never

[continues

Some poems though, appear to require little or no annotation. What might be the fiction imagined here, where everything seems on the surface, readily accessible? A poem invoking beaches once more, strands, and beach chairs, not deck chairs. There is a distinction made that requires some elucidation, unless the reader imagines the poet being just a little bit obtuse, obscure, perhaps even fey, whimsical. This is possible, and yet will have little do with the choice of term or phrase and everything to do with the fact, the object being represented in the image conjured by the words.

The beach chair has its own names, in other languages, in Danish, a *strandkurv*, in German, a *Strandkorb*, literally a beach basket, the shell or frame made of wicker. Originating in 1882, designed by Wilhelm Bartelmann, in the town of Rostock, a Hanseatic city on the River Warnow, inland from the Baltic Sea. Here, on the shores of the Baltic, and to an extent the North Sea, is where the beach basket is to be found.

So, the imagined fiction goes, there are the *strandkorb*, side by side, but far apart at the same time. This is suggestive of what? It is enough for the poet to present the image. The rest is up to the reader, who reads of a gaze, a glance, shared, and of poems. A poem that talks of the arrival of poems, the possible non-arrival of poems, as if so many postcards – the image itself one from a strand, a coastal resort – had been sent, gone awry, remaining undelivered, misdirected, or even perhaps returned to sender. A poem is not dissimilar, even though of course, it is nothing like a postcard. The question is one of analogy. Everything is there, Everything is a surface, on the surface, and yet saying something else. Or not. This is for the reader to decide, to imagine, and so invent a fiction, from what the fiction gives and withholds.

But the *Strandkorb*. Might there be a precedent? A literary source? When all else fails, reference and allusion can save the day, giving to the impertinence of the modern text an unassailable authority. There is this:

> Tony stieg behutsam durch das hohe, scharfe Schilfgras, das am Rande des nackten Strandes stand. Die Reihe der hölzernen Strandpavillons mit ihren kegelförmigen Dächern lag vor ihnen und ließ den Durchblick auf die Strandkörbe frei, die näher am Wasser standen und um die Familien im warmen Sande lagerten: Damen mit blauen Schutzpincenez und Leihbibliotheksbänden, Herren in hellen Anzügen, die müßig mit ihren Spazierstöcken Figuren in den Sand zeichneten, gebräunte Kinder mit großen Strohhüten auf den Köpfen, die schaufelten, sich wälzen, nach Wasser gruben, mit Holzformen Kuchen bucken, Tunnels bohrten, mit bloßen Beinen in die niedrigen Wellen hineinwateten und Schiffe schwimmen ließen…Rechts ragte das Holzgebäude der Badeanstalt in die See hinaus.

This, from Thomas Mann's *Buddenbrooks,* set in Lübeck, and offering scenes on the Baltic strand, offers one of the first references to the beach basket chairs, invented by Bartelmann. The novel was published in 1902, but the scene in question is set in the 1840s, when the chair had yet to be invented. This is what fiction can imagine. All at once, any annotation becomes redundant, save perhaps to point out the anachrony.

There still remains a question of translation. What do translations of the novel give as the substitute for *Strandkörbe*? John E. Woods translates this as 'wicker beach chairs'. H. T. Lowe-Porter offers 'basket-chairs'. Here are the two translations, for the purpose of comparison (this being perhaps, the excess beyond any merely conventional response to the requirement for annotation and reference):

[continues

IV.

Squall and chafe,
Torrential needles stinging cold
Anachronistic season
Out of rhyme, all reason gone
With yearning
Anticipating winter dark
The closeness of a body's warmth
And pricking at the heart
Tattoo the absence with
A rarer image, phantom faced.
My soul, well mired in
Upheaving waters,
Fret that soaks me through,
As if I were
Transparent,
Paper thin,
Blown upon the tidal, the tormenting air.

V.

Cloudlow the beach is hung,
Pressing down.
Bold pillows, air structures
Sky rounded
In the urgent breeze;
A gale too many, too much
For you to hear the whispers,
The silent orisons I send out,
As, storm warned, the seas turn,
Darker duck discolouring
Greenblue
Buffeting sand churned
To fail against the implacable, empty beach.
Gull cry, tern barracking,
Sounds that threaten
To all but crowd out the finer air
In which my only words,
The words that lack the endlessness of ocean,
Might be heard, though
Remaining, sadly, all I have to send
With less than futile hope that
Baltic currents will deliver them, timely,

[continues

First H. T. Lowe-Porter, who collaborated with Mann on her 1924 translation:
> Tony picked her way through the rushes on the edge of the beach. In front of them was a row of round-topped wooden pavilions, and beyond they could see the basket-chairs at the water's edge and people camped by families on warm sand – ladies with blue sun-spectacles and books out of the loan-library; gentlemen in light suits idly drawing pictures in the sand with their walking-sticks; sun-burnt children in enormous straw hats, tumbling about, shovelling sand, digging for water, baking with wooden moulds, paddling bare-legged in the shallow pools, floating little ships. To the right, the wooden bathing-pavilion ran out into the water.

And now, John E. Woods in 1993 (the period between translations is great in part because Lowe-Porter held exclusive rights to the translation of Mann for fifty years):
> Tony carefully waded up through the tall, sharp rushes bordering the exposed beach. And now the row of wooden beach pavilions, with their little round roofs lay before them, and beyond that, closer to the water, the wicker beach chairs with families encamped around them in the warm sand: ladies with pince-nez tinted blue and library books; gentlemen in light-coloured suits, lazily drawing figures in the sand with their walking sticks; tanned children under immense straw hats – shoveling, tumbling, digging for water, baking pies in wooden plates, burrowing tunnels, wading up to their naked knees in the low surf, sailing little ships. The large wooden swimming pier jutted out into the water on their right.

Disregarding differences between English-English of the 1920s and American-English (albeit that of an American translator who lives in Berlin), the first difficulty is in the verb 'stiegen'. Most translations indicate vertical motion, so: Tony climbed, ascended, rose, moved up. Context of course is everything (well, almost). One possible alternative translation therefore might be 'stepped'. 'Picked' side-steps the problem, while 'waded' contextualises the motion, giving Tony's action a place, rushes (or reeds, as one might translate 'Schilfgras') growing in waterbeds. There are many other small matters that present difficulties, small traces of the untranslatable, which is not particular to Mann's German (or indeed to any text in any language). And it is not my purpose to suggest an inadequacy in either translation; though it might be pointed out that Lowe-Porter avoids the translation of 'nackten' altogether (naked, bare, raw), which Woods offers as 'exposed', while Woods translates *bloßen Beinen* somewhat idiosyncratically as 'naked knees', while Lowe-Porter gives a more literal translation as 'bare legged' ('bare legs' would be equally accurate). And while the earlier translation gives *blauen Schutzpincenez* as 'blue sun-spectacles', the later provides 'pince-nez tinted blue'. The term 'tinted' is not used at all, though inferred by the colour, the context being a beach, and therefore…

But it is in the 'translation' of *blauen Schutzpincenez* that translation reaches a limit, confronting the borders of language, across which even the most assiduous reader cannot pass, unable either to incorporate the full weight of the terms, which culturally and historically would have to be 'felt'. In translation, even within the same language, there is always a remainder. Something is left behind, there is an excess beyond articulation. The French 'pince-nez' ('nose pliers' or 'pinchers', and so a 'species' of the genus 'spectacles', so to speak) becomes in German *pincenez*, German having the capability of making new words through compounding them (*Schutzpincenez* is yet another illustration of the work of the compound.

[continues

As you stand
– I see you there –
At strand's edge,
Looking, longing, waiting
In anticipation of the rain that falls
Torrential on the horizon,
Darker shadings in the Sunday morning sky.
Yet I will speak once more,
With a hope born in turmoil,
And softly, into westerlies turning north,
Across the colder currents
Of an indifferent ocean,
That you may come to find them,
And so apprehend
The word unspoken
Silent in the storm.

Yet, and this is admittedly trivial, *pincenez* can also be *der Zwicker*, eye-glass, or clippers even (given the manner of the pince-nez being fixed to the nose, this latter borrowing is not a stretch). *Schutz* alone may be translated as 'shield', 'protection', 'safeguard', 'cover', and in other ways also (guard, conservation, refuge).

> The word also plays, like a transmission, with transferential or metaphorical displacement.... there is no translation of translation. ...If one were to violate it, and one must not, one would touch the untouchable of the untouchable, namely, that which guarantees to the original that it remains indeed the original.
>
> This is not unrelated to truth. Truth is apparently beyond every possible *Übertragung* and *Überstezung*. It is not the representation correspondence between the original and the translation, nor even the primary adequation between the original and some object or signification exterior to it. Truth would be rather the *pure language* in which the meaning and the letter are no longer dissociated. If such a place, the taking place of such an event remained undiscoverable. One could no longer, even by right, distinguish between an original and a translation. ...This law collapses at the slightest challenge to a strict boundary between the original and the version, or even to the self-identity or the integrity of the original. [...]
>
> These languages relate to one another in translation according to an unheard-of mode. They complete each other, ...but no other completeness in the world can represent this one, or that symbolic complementarity. [...]
>
> The mode of intention alone assigns the task of translation. Each "thing," in its presumed self-identity (for example, bread [or a plum] *itself*) is intended by way of different modes in each language and in each text of each language. ...And since to complete or complement does not amount to the summation of any worldly totality, the value of harmony suits this adjustment, and what can here be called the accord of tongues. This accord lets the pure language, and the being-language of the language, resonate, announcing it rather than presenting it. As long as this accord does not take place, the pure language remains hidden, concealed (*verbogen*), immured in the nocturnal intimacy of the "core." Only a translation can make it emerge. ...Owing to translation, in other words, to this linguistic supplementarity by which one language gives to another what it lacks, and gives it harmoniously, this crossing of languages assures the growth of languages. ...This perpetual reviviscence, this constant regeneration... by translation, is less a revelation, revelation itself, than an annunciation, an alliance, and a promise.[...]
>
> What comes to pass... is the event of a *pas de sens*, a step of meaning / no meaning. And starting from this event, it is also possible to think the poetic or literary text that tends to redeem the lost sacred and there translates itself into its model. *Pas-de-sens*: this does not signify poverty of meaning but no meaning that would be itself, meaning, beyond any "literality." And right there is the sacred. The sacred surrenders itself to translation, which devotes itself to the sacred. The sacred [*Il*] would be nothing without translation [*elle*], and translation [*elle*] would not take place without the sacred [*lui*]; the one and the other are inseparable.
>
> Jacques Derrida

All of which is to advert to the word, the very idea. Language does not represent. This is a common mistake. It signifies arbitrarily, and by common consent. A word is sent, transmitted, received. It arrives, fails to arrive, is misapprehended, *mistranslated*. There remains, in every and any word, that which always remains to be translated, even within one language, what we mistakenly call a single language, or 'one language' (English, French, Polish, German, Latin, Dutch, etc., etc., *et ainsi, und so weiter*; no language is monolingual).

[continues

4. MIRABELKA

Mirabelka dances silently in place
Holding at bay the demons of her lover
Feeding him on fruits and jams
Telling tales of journeys
Bringing unexpected gifts
Of wide eyed laughter
She touches to the very heart
Dwelling in the moment of rarer desire.

There is no 'one language', less than a single language full and present to itself in every or any use, every language is both fragmentary, incomplete and also excessive, beyond calculation. There is, in each word, the 'remains-to-be-translated'. Far from being a mere residue, something haunting from the past of a given word, there is also that which remains. It remains to come. Or not. This 'remains-to-be-translated' may never come to be translated. The dream of a full reading, a complete translation remains precisely that: a dream, the desire for plenitude, language's closing up on itself in order to announce, to affirm and articulate 'no-more-language'. But poetry gives the lie to this dream, to which the reader of prose succumbs much more readily, insistently, mired in a belief in representation, explanation, definition, closure. That which is poetic, the poetic itself (and this is no easily understood term, being hauntingly enigmatic), is that which announces the 'remains-to-be-translated' with every word. With the arrival of every word, there is another word, and another: the *word unspoken*, unspeakable, *silent in the storm* of words.

And yet translation takes place; it must. For a word to be a word it must, in principle, be transmissible, however partially, to whatever extent that the step of meaning and no meaning oscillate in the act, the event of reading, which is also, a translation. Only a translation, a reading, can cause the sacred, the other, the alterity of the other to appear, to return, not as presentation but resonance, harmony, accord. The unheard, the silent, remains as such, but apprehended through that mode of indirection that poetry, the poetic, the literary makes possible, that which dwells, in the moment, the unexpected gift, apperceived in the silent dance, as it were, so to speak, in a perpetual reviviscence of the *pas de sens*. The poetic has this chance: of by-passing presentation in its refusal, an affirmative resistance, to give itself away. An accord has the chance, and only that, in the intimacy between the *il* and the *elle*, the *elle* and the *lui*.

PŁOMYKÓWKA

Owl, rain smothered on a lime tree branch,
Dejected before morning's creep is underway,
Watches sullenly the heron, freeze frame motions,
Stutter stepping, cutting time
In a bricolage of random shapes,
Perspectivally thrown,
Chance as the order of the world
Seen mistakenly as meaning's fitful gift.

A sharp, sour edge of light:
Herkunft, Ursprung, Abstammung
Inappropriately aid the recognition
Of the inaugural hours.
Words intruding unwarranted
To disturb the dayspring
Without surcease, familiarity deserting
Draining, to leave a desert of absences
In the middle of – what to say exactly?

       How?

              What?

A dictionary mentality comes to the rescue:
Land, Landesteil oder Ort, in dem man
Geboren und aufgewachsen
Ist oder sich durch ständigen
Aufenthalt zu Hause fühlt.

Punctuate, and so puncture, the thought.
The image soon enough washed out,
In which direction spiralling none could care,
Nor notice,
              Unless
There had, a chance's untimely birth,
Been a solitary runner, entering the gates,
To cause the heron pause, the owl its head to turn,
Who sees, uninking, the scrap of paper,
Last words, lost words, fountain pen hastily inscribed
Driven unresistant from the discarded page,
Riven from a beloved notebook,
Once crumpled, now unfurling
Come to rest by the ferrous grating
Of a storm drain.

ANIMALLEGORY

There is a dogged attempt to keep the animal at bay, in the effort to give form and so place to what is called 'the human', to attribute the search for 'home' to that which is exclusively human. Yet, the animal has no home, it does not dwell. It remains in the most radical way, in the way of etymology, to offer the radicality of a deconstruction that admits neither of the authority of origin nor the permanence of a meaning, an allegory. In writing (of) the animal, one must avoid all anthropomorphisation, and equally the assumption of some transcendence, mystical or otherwise. As soon as the animal is written (of), there is a trope, irreducible to representation, irreducible to the animal as such. For to write the animal, to speak of animal, is to speak of allegory, and to speak in allegory, to speak allegory: ἄλλος (*allos*), 'another, different, other' + ἀγορεύω (*agoreuo*) 'to speak (to the assembly)'. Thus to speak of, to the other, to speak the other, but also, by a strong reading, the other speaking, speaking otherwise. To speak 'animal', to discuss the difference between animal and human is always already to speak allegorically. As of animallegory *par* 'animal', the bird is the figure its silence in flight the excellence, the owl doubly so, erasing the trait that signal *différance* of a writing The owl writes a would determine and define. metaphorical, making world irreducible to literal or its flight, the wing impossible the distinction in much, at the same scraping the parchment as animallegory, owl time as it signs the world. As ability, of our reminds us, unknowing of this very uncanniness of inescapable unhomeliness, the in the context of the Being. 'Owl' is thus an 'animot' the barn owl, but poem, its Polish title naming English reader, to serving, it is hoped, for the estrange the relation between signifier and signified. The Polish translates as 'barn owl', but, appearing as a name, it countersigns any naturalisation or mode of representation, becoming instead a proper name, a figure of countersignature and singularity. In this small gesture of irrecuperability between tongues, I have sought to suggest how birdsong, which is a demarcation of place, territory (though not 'home'), is unavailable to human reason, and is incomparable, un-naturalisable perhaps, to the communication of human language. This difference, it is suggested in the editors' introduction to *Demenageries: Thinking (of) Animals After Derrida*, "not only undermines Descartes' well-known conception of animals as 'machines' – because they are not capable of *thinking* – but also suggests that sound is a powerful means of *deterritorialization*, in the sense of making territory 'flexible' and 'changeable'".

Animallegory: George Orwell is reputed to have been the first to use this term, though I can find no source for this apocryphal assertion. (I hasten to add this note, from an anxiety born out of the anticipated accusation of being a Derridean, a post-structuralist [sic] punster). Critics have variously employed the term – there appears no discernible origin – with reference to Orwell's fable. Orwell's tale is though not an animallegory as such, for it merely domesticates the image of the animal in order to anthropomorphise it as a shorthand and somewhat conservative, and reductive troping of human characteristics or what the Early Moderns would have called 'humours'. As such, animals are ill-served, exploited for an ideological purpose.

EN ATTENDANT QUIPROQUO

The world already waits
At twilight
On a winter's afternoon,
The sky a crepuscule
Of sympathetic shades;
The writer halts above the page,
Cossettes in a corner booth,
The darker greys of accommodating chairs
Allowing, for this time, a sempiternal instance.

Epoch in amber light; suffused, the room,
A patient ambience of time withdrawn,
Recalling, in this frame of paused reflection
Corners, cafés, comforting, cocooned.

Mirabile dictu! Comes the thought,
of Hurlothrumbo's courtship
in anticipated eagerness of snowfall –
The sky being draped, its curtain quite attendant
In that instant of the act's initiation.

Citroneta, opaque and translucent, tea light lit,
The lemon wedges float, as honey,
Gathered in the depths of a transparent cup
(what would Dryden, comes the thought,
Have found in the occasion to remark,
At length and with some wit, it must be said?),
Is stirred, a murky sediment,
Significant of a less familiar sweetness,
Dispelling sharp withdrawal of bud's retreat.

Darkling – early winter's day,
A January afternoon is passed,
Quite unobserved, save for two,
Just the one, the other and
What passes, silent semaphore,
Between.

A conspiracy of waitresses, Daughters of Mnemosyne,
Could, the tip being right, recount a choric tale
Retold in corner after corner,
Where only empty plates and cups give the game away.

LOGOS

In the beginning was

                                               ... *In het begin was*

               ... Na początku był...

       I begynnelsen var...

a thicket of notions

                               een kluwen begrippen

                   gąszcz pojęć

          et knippe av begreper

In the beginning was...

             In het begin was ...

                         Na początku było...

            I begynnelsen var...

...word...
             ... *woord* ...
     ... słowo ...

...ord...

...speech...

                                           ... *spraak* ...

        ... mowa ...
            ...tale...

...discourse...

                                             [continues

WHAT'S THE WORD?

In the Greek, where signification relies solely on context of use, Logos *can mean arithmetical ratio or musical interval* (music being mathematical and ratios specifically).

But the Greek line of *Genesis* employs both *Arché* (origin rather than beginning) and *Logos* for its formula, so that, depending on how one chooses to handle the translation, it can be said that arche-originarily, there is the interval, the pause determined by ratio and, in turn, simultaneously, determining the correct ratio of the spheres, the cosmos: the

Ἐν ἀρχῇ ἦν ὁ Λόγος, καὶ ὁ Λόγος ἦν πρὸς τὸν Θεόν, καὶ Θεὸς ἦν ὁ Λόγος

universe is a musical, mathematical composition, and arrangement of reason, which itself begins, and this is its own meaning, but is also the keystone to all meaning; thus, hence, always already there will have been an apophenic architectonics, which itself is the meaning of Being, of and in Being's becoming.

However, because of that singularity of the noun by which *Logos* makes itself known indirectly, the meaning one perceives will always be singular, never universal; one cannot therefore in any legitimate manner, speak of God, as though what goes by the noun 'god' was being or had being.

Despite this, that which is indirectly, apophatically unveiled, as through a glass darkly, as the negative proof without proof, the analogy of the possibility of the impossible (call it 'god' or 'the good' if you will), only has its chance of its *Aletheia*, in the singular and weak messianic revelation, for no discernible purpose, as a singular event, in the subject's perception of a pattern. The pattern is there, the coincidence, the synchronous, the uncanny, but its why is without comprehension, inaccessible to human reason, that which is spoken otherwise beyond reason or representation, and which is only dimly grasped in the apprehension of pattern's iterable traits.

... *discours* ...
            ... dyskurs ...

...samtale...

...reason...
... rede ...

        ... rozum ...
    ...fornuft...

...ratio...

                                      ... ratio ...

... ratio ...

...rasjonalitet...

...interval...

                                    ... *interval* ...
              ... interwał ...
...pause...

...in the beginning was
                        ... *in het begin was*
    ...na początku był

...i begynnelsen var

                                        [continues

tuario,la larga ubertate del suo ingegno.
Dique potrebbesi facilmente arbitrare,
che tale subtilitate el solerte fusore inue-
stigasse de fundere, o uero conflare una
integra catenula sencia ferruminato, fa
cendo una formula conueniente, qua-
tripartita secta, Nel cetro facto uno per
uio foramine, Nelquale intromisso el
primario anulo, & applicantise poscia
le parte informate in uno, in infinito,
uno driuo allaltro leuemete si fundera.

 Le dicte catenule sopra la mediana
corpulentia della ænea Pila æqualmen-
te deriuando, ciascuna nel extremo se
cum inuinculato retiniuano uno æreo
Chodono. Gliquali Chodoni, dal me-
dio suo uerso lo imo suo haueuano pe-
ctinate fixure. Dentro dellequale una
pilula di fino chalybe resultaua a rende-
re interclusa el tintillante sonito. Erano
questi chodoni ad exigéte proportione
dagli sofflanti uenti agitati, sopra el cor-
pulento della inane Pila conuerberaua
no & acuto el suo tinnito harmoniato
cum permixti bombi del metallino tri
gone rendeuano grato & suaue & gran-
de sono, curioso excogitato & pensicu-
latamente ritrouato, Et forsa oltra el so-
nito quale nel summo del Templo de
Hierosolyma le pendente catene cum
gli ænei uasi, gli aliti fugabondo.

 Postremamente a concludere resta
una regula per intendere tutta la dimen
sione del celeberrimo tempio. Il muro
oue erano le octo fenestre, La crassitudi-
ne sua era uno & semipede, altro tanto el
scasato, o uero quella parte che uolta-
uasi, Quello medesimo lexito degli Pi-

The singular pronoun

    het enkelvoudige voornaamwoord

Zaimek w liczbie pojedynczej

    Pronomenet i entall

are you listening | I love you

    luister je / ik hou van jou

        słuchasz | kocham cię

    lytter du/ Jeg elsker deg

MOURNING

So much to say
I don't have the heart for it today

So much to say
So much to say about what happens

This unimaginable image
Would hollow out within the infinity

From beginning to end
A failure of the will

I shall substitute a longing

No change
A sort of leap
The whole body

Something to come

An obscure, humorous conformity
So much to say

Yes
The time that was allotted
The chance to think

From the very beginning
Experience of a closeness

A nearly total affinity
Across very obvious distances
A difference
In the joyously repeated affirmation

This same agreement
Never
Does away with all those deviations

[continues

Still today, I
Do not know how to name

Never any shadow, any sign

So alone
Surviving and
So melancholy today

What can be said when it multiplies? We will all have loved

The most gaily, the most innocently
Undoubtedly

This was the necessary condition

The deep and incomparable mark

A vigilant retreat
Perhaps, perhaps
This connection of necessity
With chaos, the untimely at the very worst moment

I am going to continue
Or begin again

I'm going to have to wander all alone

And I would have tried to say
How could it do so now?

***

At first I did not know
Finally – since the question remains
Just to speak
Her gifts
Those she gave us

Those she left us
Here and there

[continues

OF LOVE AND OTHER GHOSTS

I

> Und hast die Welt gemacht. Und sie ist groß
> und wie ein Wort, das noch im Schweigen reift.
> Und wie dein Wille ihren Sinn begreift,
> lassen sie deine Augen zärtlich los…
>
> [And you have made the world. And it is great
> and as a word that still matures in silence.
> And as your will grasps its meaning,
> tenderly your eyes let it go…]

I wish to start from a place of incomprehension. Not complete incomprehension: for if this were a 'place', let us say, where I were to 'find' myself, how would I know myself to be there, all being equally incomprehensible? The very idea of total incomprehension is a hyperressential, negative ideal – a dream. It is an impossible dream wherein, though knowing nothing, I have nonetheless a certain knowledge of the absence of knowledge and, with that, the ability – such a dream! – to interpret where interpretation had stalled, had been impossible from the start. Such a dream would be *as if* I were dead, a ghost, looking on the living, on all who survive, but not being able to participate in what we call living. No, not total incomprehension then; but rather, inhabiting a certain relation to understanding, to knowledge and interpretation – *as if* I were a stranger, a foreigner or incomer who has not quite – even after so many years – accommodated himself to the feel of another's tongue in his mouth, and who therefore speaks haltingly, *as if* occasionally at a loss for words; and yet knowing all the while that even in the hesitation *there*, just at or beyond the tip of the tongue, there lay *le mot juste*, the right way to express a knowledge not yet given form but apprehended nonetheless.

So, I will begin in (from), a situation of quasi-incomprehension, occupying for a while the place of the stranger or outsider, a fiction of sorts that I enjoy maintaining, having circled briefly, perhaps anxiously, around and touching on the problem of knowledge and its limits, with two citations, the interpretation of which may well remain a problem not to be solved, even for one who claims to understand:

[continues

We find the body
And we find the book
Here and there
The witness
In the form of protest

The book
Always comes to take the place
Of the body
To become its name

Each word speaks volumes
This is all we really do
Everything takes place

"This is my body"
"Keep it in memory of me"

I will not
Be able to speak of our
Own way
Which was certainly different

Little more than
Elliptical greetings
Sometimes just a wink

Such testimonies survive
They survive us
Already they survive us
Keeping the last word
And keeping silent

The word
Held to be unbearable
This unlocatable double
The place to hold
The speech to be held
The word to be kept
Friendship breathes
Right up to expiration
Possible impossible
Friends are impossible people

[continues

> Auch zu lieben ist gut: denn Liebe ist schwer. Liebhaben von Mensch zu Mensch: das ist vielleicht das Schwerste, was uns aufgegeben ist, das Äußerste, die letzte Probe und Prüfung, die Arbeit, für die alle andere Arbeit nur Vorbereitung ist.
>
> [To love is good also: for love is difficult. For one person to love another person: that is perhaps the hardest thing that is given us, the utmost, the ultimate test and proof, the work for which all other work is but preparation.]
> – Rainer Maria Rilke

> Es ist schwer zu definieren, was Liebe ist. Nur dies weie man von ihr: In der Seele ist sie eine Leidenschaft, die herrschen will; im Geist Sympathie; im Körper nur der heimliche Drang…
>
> [It is difficult to define what love is. Only this we know of it: in the soul it is a passion that wants to rule; in the spirit, sympathy [ghost(ly) in sympathy]; in the body only the secret [*heimliche*] urge…]
> – La Rochefoucauld

All my words are another's. They come to rest in my mouth, the other tongue touching mine, while remaining other. Between the two, there is contact – and also loss; something is always lost in translation. In these two commentaries on the difficulties of loving and defining that which we call 'love' there is, it seems to me, the very crux of any project of interpretation; in relation to which we find it impossible to say whether we are on the inside or outside, seeking to gain entrance. The difficulty is rather like that of being before some gatekeeper, *as if* I were before the Law, or *as if* a stranger had entered into the most secret places in the house of Being, taken up residence there, and it remained for me to give accommodation as the final act of unconditional hospitality. *Or* say rather, that this stranger, for whom there is no name, had resided there all along, putting words in my mouth, causing me to stumble at the moment of expression, or having taken away all possibility of definition, certainty and knowledge in the face of a perception, the very experience of which had left me mute. Yet all the while, being at a loss for words by which to account for such an accommodation, I had no comprehension of what was taking place.

[continues

Impossible
What we were
For one another
As if I were
Making yet another scene
Just so as to make

Things
Last long enough
The same old story
Like a little girl
Shaken by
The irresistible joy of
Uncontrollable laughter
Even when she did not laugh

On the edge
Conscious and unconscious
Ends of laughter
Affirmation of life
Very beautiful
Unfinished Interminably

As if a sign of life
Invincible force
Modestly veiled
Insistence on anonymity
This *there*
This *right there*

Unbeknowing
Exposed three times
Seen not seeing
Distracted from the fascination

I catch myself
Still protesting
I catch myself still
I smile over this
While smiling to her
A sign of life
I'll never catch up

[continues

I knew, I know, that I do not know. In my apprehension of non-understanding there resides the possibility of being or becoming completely open to the other, that other who might always already be there and who can always return to touch me once again, to give me to understand, and to apprehend the condition of my incomprehension.

~~

I have stressed already, several times, the phrase *as if* – as if I were dead, as if I were before the law, as if a stranger had entered some house. The phrase, a translation of Kant's *als ob*, assumes the function of an idiom, hypothetical or performative in nature. Generative, it proposes, supposes, presupposes an opening onto, or a meeting with a future-conditional possibility as a fictional or narrative scenario that beyond all certain knowledge might come to be revealed, which could always arrive as some unpredictable future, some ghost or manifestation of haunting from that future. Though Kant is speaking of moral good when employing the phrase in question, can we not suggest that what is also intimated in recourse to the *as if* is that singular, difficult experience spoken of by Rilke and, equally, the difficulties of interpreting, defining, determining, of which La Rochefoucauld speaks? For love, by definition, cannot be defined. Impossible to elevate to the status of a concept, 'it' remains in the experience and perception of that which is both singular and iterable; neither absolutely singular – for how would we then apprehend love were it not in some manner capable of recurring, of revenance, however inflected by Derrida's *différance*? – nor absolutely machinic, repetitive, and therefore available for stable conceptualisation.

Love therefore admits the possibility of the limits of knowledge, and with that the impossibility of a definition or exposition in any general, universalised, essentialist or objective register. At the same time, however, in remaining apart, however close it may 'feel', love also affirms a phenomenology of silent, ghostly witness; or better, let us call this a *phainomenology*, in order that the phantom, spectre, ghost or revenant might come to appear a little more clearly: something appears, there is an apparitioning, a haunting experience to come, coming to pass, and remaining as a trace, that which haunts as memory of the other *and* as the other of memory. For what the phantom or phantasm, what the spectral other bears witness to, and for which the burden is mine, is nothing less than the limit of all hermeneutics, all interpretation. At the limit, on the tip of my tongue, there beyond which I cannot go – one falls silent. Silence figures the difficulty, the impossibility, the aporia that love conjures at the heart of the self. The Kantian *als ob* draws the line, re-marks the boundary, beyond which we cannot step, yet from which we are invited to begin once more, in the face of the experience and perception, the sensation of loss.

[continues

Reaffirmation of life
Right up to the end

***

Such questions
Must be heard
With an ear
To music
With a confident obedience
With a certain abandon
The beginning of an inaudible sentence
Like an interrupted silence
An uncompromising and punctual decision
No objection could resist it
It will have been like this
Uniquely
Once and for all

And yet I can scarcely bear the apparition
In this place

The proper name declares
The unique disappearance
Of the unique

***

We must hold fast to this evidence
To its excessive clarity
And continually return to it
As if to the simplest thing
Withdrawing into the impossible

(No) more light

It always emanated from a point
That yet was not a point
Remaining invisible in its own way
A point that I cannot locate
And I would like
To give an idea
Of what it remains for me

***

[continues

This reminds me of a colloquial English-language idiom: 'I can't define x, but I know it when I see it', we say. Two examples of this come, by chance, from literature and the law. When asked by M what he knows about gold, James Bond replies, "I know it when I see it". The second use comes from a ruling on obscenity in the US Supreme Court – a famously empirical ruling that admits a limit to knowledge and gives to us the significance of the singularity of the eyewitness. Justice Potter Stewart used the phrase in defining the 'threshold' test for obscenity in Jacobellis v. Ohio (1964). Stewart's ruling addresses the impossibility of definition and the limits of knowledge specifically: "I shall not today attempt to define the kinds of material I understand to be embraced within that shorthand description [hard-core pornography]; and perhaps I could never succeed in intelligibly doing so. But I know it when I see it, and the motion picture involved in this case is not that." Importantly, Stewart, speaking of the 1958 French film *Les Amants*, directed by Louis Malle, and starring Jeanne Moreau, can only determine hard-core pornography by constructing an argument for definition grounded in non-definition, whether in the present or a possible future. The movie is *not* this thing that remains impossible to define, and thus the definition is given indirectly.

Such negative definition has subsequently become known in American English as either the elephant or the duck test. Edge International, a law firm, defines the elephant test as the manner in which an ideal partner in a venture is known only because said partner is "a creature which is hard to describe, but instantly recognisable when spotted", the definition bemoaning its own paucity of comprehension by saying "[a]fter all, there ought to be a better way of identifying the ideal partner". In the High Court in 1998, in the case of Cadogan Estates Ltd v Morris, Lord Justice Stuart-Smith remarked of the "well-known elephant test" that it "is difficult to describe but you know it when you see it". And of course, there is the even more familiar duck test, a model of inductive reasoning first aired in 1946 by Emil Mazey, secretary-treasurer of the United Automobile Workers Union, who was reported in the Milwaukee Sentinel as having said at a union meeting, "I can't prove you are a Communist. But when I see a bird that quacks like a duck, walks like a duck, has feathers and webbed feet and associates with ducks – I'm certainly going to assume that he *is* a duck."

[continues

To keep alive
Within oneself
The best sign of fidelity
I thus secluded myself on this island
As if to convince myself
That nothing
Had come to an end
A first and a last book
A terrible fortune
Between chance and predestination
She would have liked this thought
She smiles at me at this thought
She smiles at everything
She breathes life into
And revives with pleasure

The Winter Garden photograph
The radiant invisibility of a look
Clear, so clear
As if a single volume
With which I would have
Secluded myself
On an island

As if I were finally
Going to see and know everything
Life was going to continue
As if
A point of singularity

That undresses the surface
It pierces
Strikes me
Wounds me
Bruises me

It addresses itself to me

The absolute singularity
Of the other

[continues

II

I appear to have moved some way, quite rapidly, from the question of love. I shall turn back to it shortly. At least though, it is *as if* I have all my ducks in a row and have acknowledged that the elephant is in the room, so to speak, even if, like the blind person, I am going to have to feel it out in order to apprehend it. The ghosts are already here of course; they are always with us, whether or not we know this. So then, what is given us and what is received, at those places and times where communication misses, fails, is at a loss, or passes into non-understanding? Every event, every situation, and so every experience, whether that experience be of love, of music, memory, feeling oneself to have been haunted, or touched by someone, causes in the subject a trembling through access to loss, and the perception of such; every experience of loss, every time it returns not as such but as the trace of itself, brings to bear the memory of an 'itself' that is no longer; such events, situations, experiences, at the same time as they defy understanding or knowledge, absolute comprehension and definition, nevertheless require of each of us that we

> …create an appropriate mode of exposition, … invent the law of the singular event…and, at the same time, to make *as if* this… will determine the [subject] who will learn to read (to 'live') something he or she was not accustomed to receiving from anywhere else. One hopes that he or she will be reborn differently, determined otherwise as a result.

Each experience, if it is one worthy of being called an event, *will have in it* that which is transformative; its necessity will move me, even though I do not fully understand what is taking place, even though it might create confusion or appear undecidable, *as if* this were a first time, as if one had never known the meaning of a word, or all that gives the word significance, until now.

Making manifest or restoring meaning rests on a presupposition: that meaning can in some manner be stabilised, and may be made distinct, perhaps free, from perceptions. The assumption of, or the quest for, meaning harbours a dream of a science of knowledge, a methodology or mode of repeatable measurement, equal to the task. Meaning though is always, or almost always, a question of interpretation. Meaning we might say is the answer to the question put by interpretation; it is a completion, a conclusion, that which will put an end to the emptiness that interpretation implies, something that might come to 'restore' where apparently a loss, a lack is discovered.

[continues

Addresses itself
To me

A Latin word exists
To designate this wound
The word suits me all the better
Punctum

***

It is within us but not ours
What looks at us may be indifferent
Loving, dreadful, grateful
Attentive, ironic, silent
Bored, reserved, fervent
Or smiling
A child already quite old
Two infidelities, an impossible choice

On the one hand
Not to say anything
To remain silent

Or in counterpoint
To be content with just quoting

On the other hand
Avoiding all quotation
All identification
So that what is addressed
Truly comes from the other
Risks making disappear again
We are left then
With having to do and not do
Both at once

***

La chambre claire
The naïve attitude of her hands
Without either showing or hiding herself
There should not be

[continues

For many, interpretation rests on an assumption of stability, desired as a goal to be brought about. With, or leading to, that is another assumption: in interpretation, a representation may be realised, or otherwise may be *a priori* the ground of interpretation and back to which interpretation will lead as the closing of a hermeneutic circle. Hermeneutics is driven by a desire, if I can put it like this, for what Paul Ricœur calls "a demystification, …a reduction of illusion"; suspicious from the start, it nonetheless wishes to entertain, receive, restore that which had been occluded, remained secret, and which therefore must be brought to light.

[continues

There should not be
Any metonymy in this case
For love protests against it
Without either showing or hiding herself
According to the most gentle passivity
She neither shows nor hides herself

The possibility of this impossibility derails
Shatters all unity
This is love
The lure and fascination of the Sirens

I cannot really describe here
An a priori mourning
Rich in possibility
A whole experience of absence
I cannot really describe here

Those whom we knew, met, loved
Impossible, indecent, unjustifiable
What long ago
More or less secretly
Resolutely
I had promised myself never to do

But then what? Silence
Another wound, another insult
A piece of myself
Like a piece of the dead
The having been

I will not be able to carry it out
The promise of return
To go on speaking of this
All alone
After the death of the other
An endless insult or wound
And yet also a duty
Always the promise of return

***

Today someone brought me a note

[continues

III

What I am suggesting is that the experience of what, for the sake of argument, might be called provisionally the event of love – and with that one might add the experience of music, as being amongst the most inner, private of experiences, subjective perception being barely communicable to others directly – comes to arrive in a ghostly fashion to my perception. No hermeneutic model can account for this. Psychologism is woefully inadequate also. Though I cannot say with any certainty what these experiences are, I know them when I feel them, if not see them. Before any rigorous reflection by which I believe I distance myself from the world, and so distrust my intimate relation with that, there is the primacy of perception, which is groundless, though encountered as mediated sensibility in apprehension.

Let us recall La Rochefoucauld, who in the *Reflections* also observes that 'true love is like seeing ghosts; we all talk about it, but few of us have ever seen one'. We might pause to reflect on the proximity *and* distance in the mind/body dualism in the passage that he acknowledges around the determination of love. What is implicit in the French original becomes more pointedly available in its German translation: "Es ist schwer zu definieren, was Liebe ist. Im Geist Sympathie; im Körper nur der heimliche Drang…" *Geist* on the one hand, *Körper* on the other, and between these supposedly discrete locations – to which the phenomenology of Merleau-Ponty has given the lie more explicitly than Husserl – we find the tracing of sympathy. There is a transfer, or motion and passage in sympathy or empathy or compassion. In sympathy I suffer your experience, I suffer with you; it is, in my perception *as if* that which you feel I feel in spirit. There is also that secret urge, so secret that it is at the heart of the self, in what Heidegger would call the house of Being. The separation, Cartesian in nature, will not hold. For if the sympathy I feel is analogous, I believe, with that which the other feels for me, then indirectly, I apperceive that which is secret, hidden in the other. In this *allegory* I am proposing there is the image of the unreadable and inexpressible, but wherein there comes the trace we call 'sensation', the 'real' of perception according to Husserl. I therefore experience that which is other within me, *as if* I had access to the other's most secret desire. In the apperception of this ghostly sympathy or solicitude is that which traverses all borders *as if* there passed between us in the analogical apperception, the other having entered secretly into ourselves. I remain on the verge, hovering, though I cannot define this; and the very affirmation is traced in the idea of love; becoming speechless, falling into silence and at a loss for words yet being what is called 'in love', finding myself moreover to have fallen 'in love' – or rather having been taken in love, by love, love of the other – I find myself always already apprehended, invaded.

[continues

That was yesterday
Another strange coincidence
The impossible utterance
Revenant à la lettre
The sentence of the *I*
The time of this elliptical sentence

Between
The possibility and impossibility
Syntax of time
Something like imminence
Absolute silence

Nothing more to be said

This air that becomes
More and more dense
More and more haunted
It is inevitable
Both just and unjust

Choosing clothes
Contrapuntal theory

[continues

That secret urge, *heimliche Drang*: is it mine, or the other's? Whose 'urge' calls, whose 'responds'? The questions are far from idle, for while there is my corporeal presence in the world, there is also that self, the other 'I' or what Merleau-Ponty calls 'my seeing body' in order to distinguish it from the 'body as a visible thing'. If there is sympathy, and if it is of the spirit (ghostly), then, unbounded, without limit, unbounded by any definition according to all models of knowledge, classical or negative, does it not speak of a transport between self and other; and with that, a translation of self and other, self into other, something having got past the border guards, as it were? Is this what is so secret and yet so familiar, homely, the *heimliche* become *heimische*? Is that other I think of as external to me, not already 'subtended'? I am tempted to run the risk of gesturing toward some strong readings of this phrase on which I am touching, offering improper translations while remaining in one language, naming in another's tongue without fully comprehending in the name of love here, and thereby committing acts of loving transport, transmission, traduction, translation and betrayal (*translatus, transferre, trans+ducere*) that take place, coming to pass in the unnameable trace or trait. These acts treat of that which is so hard to define that, like a thief, it breaks down the barriers and limits of knowledge, rational thought, any merely hermeneutic quest, causing such a quest to run against the limits of its own efforts at restoration or reconstruction. In the word *Drang* there might be whispered, written secretly *Trieb*, but equally, perhaps, *Antrieb, Impuls, Anwandlung, Stimmung, Auflage, Eindruck* or *Sehnsucht*, all of which open the revelation of the impossibility of any ground, except for the sense of Being haunted by the *Ab-grund*, formed by the ghostly in the self, and with that, once more a perception of the loss that haunts all Being.

And there is loss, precisely because while my corporeal condition is always an 'adherent to *location* and to the *now*' the Being, my 'seeing body', the self subtended, is always both flux and matrix: of memory, sensation, perception, of all that has come to pass and is no more and all that is yet to come. With such loss – and here I think is that which haunts La Rochefoucauld and Rilke equally – comes a silence. At the limits of speech or writing, on the tip of my tongue, I founder. Loss, like love, can render us silent on the face of things. This is why love is hard. Not simply hard to define, but just hard, difficult, as Rilke observes: it is the most difficult gift we are given, the hardest work, a remark of the poet's that echoes Freud's belief that mourning is the most difficult, if not the only 'real' work we must pursue, never knowing if we do this correctly. Love is difficult perhaps because within its gift is the promise of loss, the falling silent of the other, whom I survive, to whom there can no longer be anything said, but who remains in the passage of innumerable traces that have the ghostly possibility to return in that silence which haunts touchingly at that place called by Rilke the 'speechless heart' – 'Im sprachlosen Herzen' Such a writing on the part of the other is admitted by Rilke in another poem, 'Die Stille':

[continues

Procession of stigmata
A wound comes
In (the) place of the point
Signed by singularity
In (the) place of its very instant
In (the) place of this event
Place is given over
For the same wound
To substitution
Which repeats itself here
Retaining of the irreplaceable
Only a past desire.

Anamnesis
Even if it breaks off
Always too soon
Promises itself
Each time
To begin again
It remains to come

…

I turn to you today
In the end
I wasn't able to write

Intractable intensity
Bodily struggle
With language
In language
Left living in me
A friendship of which I have shown myself
To be unworthy

Why do
Just the right words
Escape me here?
Fatigue
False emergencies
Frantic running around

Living
At an absurd pace
We were parting

[continues

> Der Abdruck meiner kleinsten Bewegung
> bleibt in der seidenen Stille sichtbar.
>
> [The imprint of my smallest motion
> remains visible in the silken silence].

The intimate proximity Rilke imagines in 'Die Stille' is all the more marked for the disappearance or invisibility of the beloved, in a poem where love is to be heard but not seen:

> Hörst du Geliebte, ich hebe die Hände –
> hörst du: es rauscht…
> […]
> Hörst du Geliebte, ich schließe die Lider
> und auch *das* ist Geräusch bis zu dir.
> Hörst du, Geliebte, ich hebe sie wieder…
> …aber warum bist do nicht hier'
>
> [Listen, love, I lift my hands –
> listen: there's a rustling…
> […]

[continues

On a train platform
Our last meeting

Distraction, diversion
Means of escape
Some other thing
Puts me at a loss
For just the right words
This being at a loss
This impossible mourning

That nevertheless remains
Endlessly hollowing out
The depths of our memories

A meeting in a café
A letter eagerly torn open
A burst of laughter
Revealing the teeth
A tone of the voice
An intonation on the phone

A parting in
A train station
This being at a loss

I have often felt this loss
I have already lost
I lack the strength to speak
To recall
Each time
Another end of the world

The same end
Another
Every future anterior

This with no other beginning
Than the rending cry
That separates from birth
To try to the very end
On the very edge
On the fold that marks

[continues

> Listen, love, I close my eyes,
>
> and even *that* makes sounds to reach you.
>
> Listen, love, I open them again…
>
> but why are you not here?].

The beloved, the other, is thus doubled, divided, impossibly close, closer than oneself to oneself *and* distant, having the distance of absolute limit, horizon or boundary simultaneously. Loss and silence are felt from within the very intensity of love, the place where love's revenance reveals itself, the other being both "Nur die ich denke: Dich / seh ich nicht" [Only her of whom I think: You / I cannot see']. The gap between knowing and unknowing, between what can be grasped and expressed and what is inexpressible, ineffable, undecidable, remains an aporia.

It is there too in that questioning anxiety that haunts the opening line from Rilke's first *Duino Elegy*: "Wer wenn ich schriee, hörte mich den aus der Engel / Ordnungen?" [Who, if I cried, would hear me amongst the order of angels?]. No direct response is possible of course; no answer comes. All the poet can offer is the apperception that beauty is nothing but the beginning of terror, which we can just barely endure. The absolute limit is here; no understanding can account for the singular experience. All one can do, in the event, is bear witness to that which cannot be resolved, the impossible, the undecidable itself. As Rilke continues to observe, in a remark that speaks directly to the limits of the sayable:

> …wir nicht sehr verläßlich zu Haus sind
>
> in der gedeuteten Welt.
>
> [we are not very dependably at home
>
> in the interpreted world]

[continues

Keeps
The trace of this rending
For fear of being seized
Submerged, reengulfed

Right here
Almost at random
Silences of the same forgetting
Faces of memory
That we do not wish to see
Our mourning endures
But cannot possibly want
The unbearable and yet
Endured certainty

The *without return* is necessary
In order to give *Rien que pour voir*

Vocabulary gathers
Sometimes condenses, intensifies
So to speak
Its density

Yes
An intense desire
To begin again now
I will do so
As if I could still hope to surprise

On the other side
A cry or a song
Perpetual coming
The share of darkness in a voice
I know
I can still hear very distinctly
As if I were
Finally
Going to see this voice
On the other side
From the side of the body
Not far from some source
But also the fall
The fall

[continues

All we can therefore do is give ourselves attentively, in sufferance, awaiting the arrival of the other, in silence:

> Stimmen, Stimmen. Höre, mein Herz...
> [...]
> Nicht daß du *Gottes* ertrürtre
> die Stimme, bei weitem. Aber das Wehende höie,
> die ununterbrochene Nachricht, die aus Stille sich bildet.

> [Voices, voices. Listen, my heart...
> [...]
> Not that you could endure
> the voice of God, no, not by far. But hear the fluttering,
> the continuous message that forms itself out of silence.]

With the insistent rhythm of chant, with that call and response traced between the 'voices' and the injunction to the heart that it hear, and thus respond, to a silence in which – out of which – the expression of the other is carried, Rilke figures an invisible exchange. The iterability of tone or voice is taken up within the alliteration, as the first line of the passage installs a performative openness in itself: one that, arguably, cannot be closed, completed.

[continues

The torrent

***

Who could ever speak?
Who would already know?
Enduring this work
From the very start
The impossible
     Interminable
                   Inconsolable
                                  Irreconcilable

An entire way of thinking
A recrudescence intensified

Let us continue
Let us pause

The question is repeated
But what might this mean?

I am going to have to break off
There is not enough time
A bit more time
To say 'I am dead'

This incredible grammar
This impossible time
This impossible tense
The strange time
Grammatical monstrosity

Without saying more
In us
We are naming space
We are speaking

Visibility of the body
Geometry of gazes
Memories or monuments
Memory of visible scenes

                                                               [continues

Rilke has installed in the word, as possibility of the word, all that might come to touch, but which, being below the skin of the visible word, remains silent, lost from mere sight, and immanent, always to come, if we open ourselves to the other's voice.

Not God then but God's voice, God's tone or pitch; a mood, atmosphere, feeling, that which befalls me, taking me by surprise, felt but impossible to present directly – a silent music, *as if* such a thing, the very idea, apparently paradoxical, were possible. Being must always be touched by loss, and this can only be felt in the significance of silence, wherein all remains unknown but with the possibility of knowing, even or perhaps especially if that knowledge may never arrive. Love attests to this – as does music when it touches, if it touches, and where any given musical work may touch you, but not me; or you and me but not a third. Unable to speak of music in anything but the briefest of manners, I raise it here as a possible analogy for the work of love, as that which can touch but which cannot be conveyed in the experience as such. You might hear but not be moved by Bach's unaccompanied cello suites for example, even though I might find them almost unbearably touching, as I do Schubert's *Winterreise*; and too, though differently, Dido's aria from Purcell's opera of *Dido and Aeneas*, 'When I am laid in earth'. It is not in the music itself therefore that whatever touches and leaves me speechless is to be found. Neither is it solely in 'me'; for this experience is not programmable, repeatable; the coming, the apparitioning of the revenant cannot be guaranteed. Nor is the experience of what is figured in the name of love, by which one finds oneself touched, and which in memory can return as both the phantom of that touch and the loss of any material experience. Were I to attempt to explain or understand what we call love, I might fall into mistaking the 'who' for the 'what', and so miss the mark.

What I *can* say is that God's voice – if there is any – remains undecidable, available neither to cataphasis nor apophasis. The ruse of the name, a complex siglum, gestures in the place of any presence, any knowledge, once more, to an endless opening, to that which opens abyssally at the ends of knowledge. Silence, loss, absence: none of these attests either with any certainty of knowledge, the promise of an understanding that, once reached, may bring a stability, or the rigour of an interpretative hermeneutics to a meaning or presentation – positive and restorative or negative and determining. Apperception of the other is *just* that sense I receive, if it comes, and by which I might be opened, in the event of having been turned in Derrida's words "toward a past *and* toward a future that are as yet unpresentable". What is traced through Rilke's poetry is this temporal and ghostly continuity – 'ghostly' inasmuch as, being the trace of that alterity apperceived through love (itself already a trace), it remains unavailable to any ontology, but nevertheless makes itself sensed, even if only expressed through what appears on the surface a mystical discourse.

[continues

No longer anything but

Images of the other
One who has

        Disappeared

Passed away
Leaving in me
Only images

I am
An image for the other

Am looked at
With all the love
Of someone
Who at the moment of dying
Looks out from within us
From now on
More than ever
We bear in ourselves
The gaze that bears on us
Infinitely
Far away in us

In us
Limitless enlargement
The experience of this time
We will never have the time
Right up to the
Final interruption
Fantastic aporia
We will never have the time

***

To rethink childhood
I feel at such a loss
Left speechless
Absence forever unthinkable
The unthinkable itself
In the depths of tears
In my heart and in my thought

[continues

Rilke's poetry touches – I will not say it touches 'us', I will not assume a shared experience – because in what Paul de Man has defined as its daring, its affirmation and promise figured in the materiality of poetry itself, the poet realises for the good reader the extent to which "[n]either love nor the imagining power of the deepest nostalgias can overcome the essential barrenness of the self and of the world.... Rilke's figure of humanity", is given not in an image of the self but through the poetic performative, the continuous utterance of Being grasping its sense of loss, of being constantly at the limit of comprehension, and feeling in the sensate apprehension of love the merest sign of affirmation.

Thus, de Man asserts, Being in Rilke is figured as "the frailest and most exposed creature imaginable". Language *is* that affirmation, the (a)materiality of the word our only clew, to make us hear, to make us feel. (The word, as clew, as trace, can be recorded as both sound and inscribed sign on a page or a screen. It can make us hear therefore. But apophatically, the trace upon a page or screen can cause us to hear the phantasmic voice of the one who wrote that silent mark, even though this other is absent, far away, or dead.)

So we arrive at that which is written at the inner limit of words, and which signals 'toward a past *and* toward a future that are as yet unpresentable'. I may feel, in my heart, via that which I believe to have come to touch me, that there has been a trace, necessarily – the idea that it has not yet arrived has, of necessity, to bear within it the possibility that it will arrive – and, equally, that in the future there will have been a trace. Words do not cover the loss; they do not replace the silence – quite simply, in their flow, they give place to the indirect disclosure of loss and silence, often through the trope of love. Silence, in this understanding, remains the possibility of sound, of speech, a declaration, some whisper. Silence thus "remains a modality of speech: a memory of promise and the promise of memory". If *there is* some silence, some loss, these, and the sense by which they are revealed, are not simply negatives. For in their institution of negatives – absence of sound, absence of presence, full being, the presence of the other – there in the apprehension of loss, silence, the negative must deny itself as a determined negative; the negation, Derrida observes, "denies itself. It de-negates itself". Only on this impossible possibility, only in the modality of some "secret denial" can the name be spoken, can the other call, at some border, boundary, edge or limit, unavailable otherwise to the "order of the sensible".

[continues

A friendship
At once tender and mocking
At once light and serious
Cutting laughter
Which I always loved
All the paths
On which we crossed
Remain
Forever uninterrupted

Childhood and tears
Surviving
Forevermore bereft
Who could ever venture
Without trembling?
To sign might seem impossible.

Unless a certain experience

Of 'we', of 'yes', 'yes we'

Like a drifting aphorism
A shared signature
Il n'y aura pas de deuil

And so let us dream
An apocalyptic repetition
Hidden or playful
Elusive memory
Spectral echo
Clandestine and visionary
It conspires in the exhalation
Respires or breathes

I would have followed
Let myself be led
I did not know how to take this
Today
I do not know any better
I still do not know
I cannot stop looking
It holds me
It will not let me go
The terrible condition
The thought of the worst
You will not let go
The worse appears a second time

[continues

IV

What I love, who I love, can only ever come to appear at the limit, where reason, knowledge and analysis fail. There might thus appear the sign of being 'in tune' with another, a harmony between two, to recall *Stimmung* and *Stimmen*. Karlheinz Stockhausen has observed of *Stimmung* that all possible meanings resonate in the word, incorporating for the composer 'the meanings of the tuning of a piano, the tuning of a voice, the tuning of a group of people, the tuning of the soul', of people being 'in a good *Stimmung*' I have attempted to show this spectral relation through Rilke briefly, and more broadly in the condition of the subject's existence as a 'singularity *always in relation*'. That *always* must be qualified: relation comes to appear, touch takes place, and words, understanding, meaning, are found wanting, in the event of love befalling us, in the experience of loss, in the touch that music can effect. Poetry also has the power to achieve a performative figuration of the relation, the 'harmonic' inflection or resonance within the word. Love is thus given, in, through, the risk of the trace, in the condition, the bearing of language. Poetic language thus gives itself, gesturing toward (in the act of figuring performatively) a past and that which is to come.

Love and music are such expressions, because even in their loss and silence – the very idea of which is terrifying – there remains the perception of the 'persistence of the possibility of relation'. In receiving the other, finding oneself open, taken up in what John Caputo calls a "fluctuating play in which things are never reducible to what they are" and "where the bottom drops out, where the surface opens up, where shadowy formations replace the rock-hard identities of being and presence.... One begins to sense the abyss within.... The look of the other draws us into the mystery, shakes our naïve belief in surfaces, shapes... self-identity and the steadiness of presence." I survive therefore, in the promise of remaining haunted by that which – though it is irreducible to any meaning, unavailable to any presence, resistant to any meaning – comes to determine me most urgently nonetheless. I live in the other, touched all the more intensely, immediately for unveiling the ghostly trace of the loss and silence that are ultimately my own, for all the contradiction that this implies.

[continues

I know the debt that binds me
I will not even begin
To give an account of this debt

I am not able here
To recall all the places
Occasions people thoughts and words
That will have kept us together

To this day
Together apart
Together dispersed into the night
Invisible to one another
This being together no longer assured

You remain
For me
In a certain way
Forever unknown and infinitely secret

I am sure of it
With a faith
Nothing attests to this better
Than the fact that I want to speak
Later perhaps
This very time

This future
Announces the attestation
Of a right to say we

As if
To take up an interrupted conversation
To follow a thread of memory
More or less obscurely
Woven together silently

The thread
The event
The destination
To whom it happens
Tangled web of these threads
Our secret language
I approved in silence
We reserve ourselves
A kind of grammatical contraband
The shibboleth of a hidden intimacy
Clandestine, coded, held back
Discretely held in reserve
Held in silence
What was said and left unsaid

[continues

To conclude then: on the tip of my tongue, in that experience and perception for which I have no words, for which I cannot account, because no measure is possible, I lose myself and admit the other. As Derrida observes, "I am never more haunted by the necessity of dying than in moments of happiness and joy. To feel joy and to weep over the death that awaits are for me the same thing." Love is just the name for this haunting feeling, and so the sign of the threshold from where one must start, once again, beyond any false dream of restoration, or the search for an illusory closure.

If there is manifestation at all, if there is the apparition at all it is in this: in the being touched most intensely *and* apprehending indirectly absolute alterity. To be as faithful to the other as I can means risking not closing or completing the interpretive circle but to remain open, remain in a relation of incomprehension with regard to the other.

Silenced, you, in this unsaid, you

You will have surrounded me
Besieged me in advance
Leaving the chance without the possibility of deciding
Private cryptic
Interrupted
You drop a stitch
Interrupted
I lose a thought
With you and me it's decisive

I suffer so much
Not being able
For lack of time
Rushing as I must
Toward the posthumous we
It is in the last breath
I still do not know
I do not know how
My fragments will
Have only made things worse
Nothing will silence
The always open risk
As always
The only one
Worse than the worst

What happens when one thinks an impossibility?
Is this possible?
So close to the experience of the worse
Does the experience of the impossible

Become possible?
What possibility is there?
The hyperbole of we

This survives
It survives as survival
A subtle infinitesimal excess
A beautiful risk to run
There it is
As if for the first time in my life
There it is
This is what
I tell myself today
What I would have wanted
To try to tell you

Let us listen

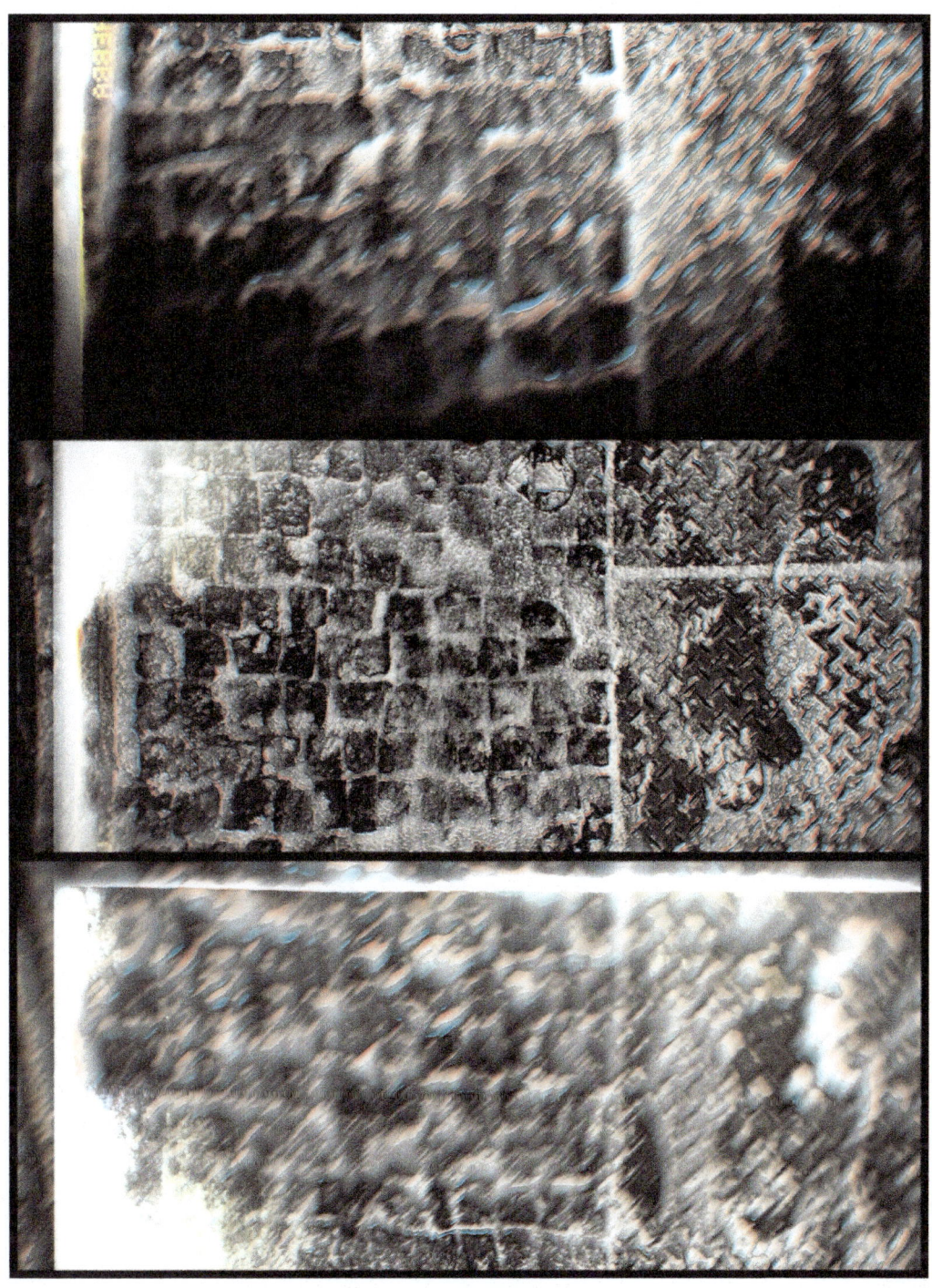

AFTERWORD

Rubus idaeus / Hyacinthus orientalis (Raspberry and Hyacinth)

> Rushing as I must
> Toward the posthumous we
> It is in the last breath
> I still do not know
> I do not know how
> My fragments will
> Have only made things worse
> Nothing will silence
> The always open risk

Julian Wolfreys has played with the notion of a posthumous We – are we not posthumous as soon as we write? – by calling up a famous line from *The Waste Land*: "These fragments I have shored against my ruins". Eliot's draft shows that he had initially written: "These fragments I have spelt into my ruins". He added above the line: "shored against" (*The Waste Land: Facsimile*, p. 80), which presents something like a riddle, for the two versions convey widely different meanings.

The first version can be construed as: 'My poem made up of fragments will spell my name, write my words on my ruins'. The revision adds the meaning of 'propping up, supporting'. This time, the poetic fragments are called upon to ward off an impending ruin. In the first concept, the poet's task is to mobilize the "withered stumps of time" (*The Waste Land*, line 104) so as to transmute them into the poet's signature. Thus the poem will offer itself as a ruined monument, capable of surviving among the ruins of a Culture laid waste by the War.

In the second concept, the poem provides a rampart of words, a tentative construction, prosthetic props helping a wounded poet survive after having witnessed the destruction, material and moral, brought about by European madness. Such madness has not abated, and it entails that We is always posthumous, a We surviving among ruins, a ruined We.

Whether ruins should be construed as negative or positive, what stands out is that there is a tension between Eliot's traditionalist view of culture as a series of 'monuments' arranged in an 'ideal order' and those hauntingly ruined monuments. In the line itself, Eliot's syntax balances a deictic 'these', which testifies to an objective existence of the poem, and a possessive 'my'. Even if there are ruins, even if these words, grammatical subjects and cultural landscapes out there, are all in ruins, they are *my* ruins.

Ruins thus offer the only 'true refuge', as Beckett repeated in his later prose texts. Ruins combine reminders of a pathetic past and memories of petrified horrors. In a ruin, the monuments are half-dead only, suggesting that one can die there and then be reborn. The ruin, freezing ancient joys and new tragedies, is stuck between two deaths, the death of the cultural heritage and the demise of the observer, whose sure and certain agony has been monumentalized long in advance: longing and nostalgia, mourning and empathy, grandiose decay of the old Ego and cheap selfies in tainless mirrors, faded epiphanies and vociferous tragedy.

Lacan presented *Antigone* as the paradigm of tragedy because in that famous play ethics and esthetics were knotted together by the concept of a 'second death' allegorised in the heroine's condemnation to be buried alive. In *Oedipus at Colonnus*, the chorus had stated that it would be better "not to be" (*me phynai*, line 1224), or 'never to have been born' than continue living. Non-being would be preferable to endless suffering, a stark and dark notion that can be only lightened and enlightened by a *Witz,* such as this joke recalled by Freud: "'Never to be born would be the best thing for mortal men.' 'But' adds the philosophical comment in *Fliegende Blätter,* 'this happens to scarcely one person in a hundred thousand.'"[1] What if the posthumous We was that One in a hundred thousand?

Draping the Sky… invokes Eliot more than Freud in jagged and open lines that bring us beyond the divide between life and death so as to usher in another site in which the posthumous We happens; it happens by positing on the page a layered syntax of rewriting that is as witty as touching. Here is another example, a recreation of the Hyacinth girl section of the *Waste Land,* more homage than parody:

> I shall call you
> Raspberry girl
> Fruits drenched in rain drops
> Laughing eyes
>   celadon in hue
> (a wash, a tint, a trick
>   of morning light
>   thunder's refraction
> and the daylight yellowed)
>
> And you will cause my words
> To fail once more
>   as
> I look into the heart of light,
> In silence I know nothing
>
> And am consumed

After Eliot's poem, Wolfreys takes us to a point of pathos beyond life and death. Here is the original passage, in which an unnamed man addresses a young woman called 'the hyacinth girl':

> —Yet when we came back, late, from the Hyacinth garden,
> Your arms full, and your hair wet, I could not
> Speak, and my eyes failed, and I knew neither
> Living nor dead, and I knew nothing,
> Looking into the heart of light, the silence.
>
>   (*The Waste Land,* lines 37-42)

Poetry makes us look into the heart of light and thus enacts the experience of a survival beyond the binaries of silence and music, sun and moon, light and dark, beyond immense collective death and tenuous future life leaping and speaking in the plural as a We. Such a 'We' needs another, and it could be you, it could be me:

> Crossing borders,
>   One tongue in the mouth of another.

Jean-Michel Rabaté

---

[1] Sigmund Freud, *Jokes and Their Relation to the Unconscious,* trans. James Strachey, Norton, 1989, p. 65.